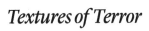

Textures of Terror

California Series in Public Anthropology

The California Series in Public Anthropology emphasizes the anthropologist's role as an engaged intellectual. It continues anthropology's commitment to being an ethnographic witness, to describing, in human terms, how life is lived beyond the borders of many readers' experiences. But it also adds a commitment, through ethnography, to reframing the terms of public debate—transforming received, accepted understandings of social issues with new insights, new framings.

Textures of Terror

THE MURDER OF CLAUDINA ISABEL VELÁSQUEZ AND HER FATHER'S QUEST FOR JUSTICE

Victoria Sanford

 UNIVERSITY OF CALIFORNIA PRESS

The publisher and the University of California Press Foundation gratefully acknowledge the generous support of the Barbara S. Isgur Endowment Fund in Public Affairs.

University of California Press
Oakland, California

© 2023 by Victoria Sanford

Parts of the introduction and chapter 1 are adapted from Victoria Sanford, "From Genocide to Feminicide: Impunity and Human Rights in Twenty-First Century Guatemala," *Journal of Human Rights* 7, no. 2 (2008): 104–22, https://doi.org/10.1080/14754830802070192. https://www.tandfonline.com.

Cataloging-in-Publication Data is on file at the Library of Congress.

ISBN 978-0-520-39345-5 (cloth : alk. paper)
ISBN 978-0-520-39346-2 (ebook)

Manufactured in the United States of America

32 31 30 29 28 27 26 25 24 23
10 9 8 7 6 5 4 3 2 1

For Jorge
and
In Memory of Claudina Isabel

Contents

Acknowledgments

This book has been a labor of love. It has been my honor to accompany Jorge Rolando Velásquez Durán in his quest for justice for his beloved Claudina Isabel. I thank him for his trust, friendship, and perseverance.

I thank the survivors who shared their most private experiences with gender violence and their struggles to survive and protect their children.

I thank the many human rights advocates and justice operators in Guatemala and in exile who risk their lives every day to improve the life chances of their compatriots. I especially thank Carlos Pop, Amílcar Méndez, Ana María Méndez Dardón, Carolina Escobar Sarti, Lucrecia Molina Theissen, Claudia Paz y Paz, Aura Elena Farfán, Juan Francisco Sandoval, Thelma Aldana, Rosalina Tuyuc, Norma Cruz, Bernardo Caal, María Maquín, Jesús Tec, Gloria Elvira Reyes Ixtumul, Ana Lopez, Freddy Pecerrelli, Olga Alicia Paz, and Iduvina Hernández. Many thanks to the award-winning publisher Raúl Figueroa Sarti and F&G Editores for righteously defending free speech and for excellence in editorial, bibliographic, and technical support. Thanks also to Miriam Méndez, Rocío Méndez, and Vicente Chapero, as well as Andrea, Mercedes, Ana, Estuardo, and Erick. Guatemalan colleagues Margarita Carrera,

Edelberto Torres-Rivas, and Sam Colop are remembered and missed.

My forensic and investigator colleagues Dr. Reinhard Motte, Dr. Heather Walsh Haney, Dr. Kenneth Cohrn, June Gallant, and Dr. Leyla Renshaw generously provided pro bono assistance to human rights cases and shared their expertise with me. Working out of the spotlight, their research and documentation makes prosecutions possible. I would like to recognize the significant contributions made by the late Dr. Clyde Snow, the late Dr. Vincent Stefan, and the late Detective Greg Smith who set a high bar for us to follow.

My colleagues at Lehman College and the Graduate Center, City University of New York (CUNY), have provided excellent support, especially Louise Lennihan, William P. Kelly, Ryan Raaum, Jeff Maskovsky, Ellen DeRiso, Deborah Dwork, the late Eric Weitz, Elissa Bemporad, Danielle Zach, Yuri Gorokovich, Kenneth Schlesinger, Salah Noueihed, Michael Buckley, Janet Munch, Raymond Diaz, Alison Lehner-Quam, Deborah Rhem-Jackson, Donna Zavattiere, Pamela Mills, Eileen Markey, Shawn Plant, Migdio Dominguez, Yves Dossous, Orlando Lorca, Rachel Daniell, Joan Camilo Lopez, Jennifer Sugg, Cristina Finan, Karine Avila, Urieke Brown, and Yesenia Aviles.

Support from the John Simon Guggenheim Foundation, the International Women's Program of the Open Society Foundation, and the US Fulbright Program supported chunks of time for research and writing. The Lehman Professor of Excellence Award, the George N. Shuster Fellowship, and the CUNY Professional Staff Congress and Lehman College Faculty Development awards provided the needed in-between research support and vital course release for writing.

Over the years, I have had the good fortune to share my work in progress with friends and colleagues. Their feedback and encouragement have kept me moving forward. I am especially grateful to Asale

Angel Ajani, Nela Navarro, Alexander Hinton, Stacey Engels, Tatiana Devia, Iván Velásquez, Andy Spahn, Karen Musalo, Dorian Caal, Julie Abbott, Phyllis and Cris Beech Giraldo, Amira Thoron, Gustavo Rojas, Nhorys Torregroza, Nery Castillo, Christa Salamandra, Dagmar Herzog, Fazil Moradi, Katerina Stefatos, Kathleen Dill, Sofía Duyos, Rosario Cuevas, Mike Anastario, Michelle Bellino, Holly Dranginis, Micheline Marcom, June Erlick, Debra Rodman, Michael Bosia, Yazier Henry, Daniel Zingale, Rebecca Root, Sarah Danielsson, Shannon Drysdale Walsh, Alcira Forero Pena, Raz Segal, Chelsea Abbas, Bonnie Abaunza, Marisa Gisele Ruiz Trejo, Christelle Taraud, Rachel Seider, Aída Hernández, Teresa Sierra, Shannon Speed, Lynn Stephen, Joanne Rappaport, Alyssa Butler, Antonia Rodríguez, John Wallach, Wolf Gruner, Terry Karl, Carlos Aguirre, Antonius Robben, Richard Wilson, Daniel Rothenberg, Betsy Konefal, Roddy Brett, Philippe Bourgois, Arturo Arias, Natasha Zaretsky, Victoria Sekula, Michelle Sekula, Sally Stein, Heather Teague, Leonardo Crippa, Miho Omi, Pamela Calla, and Margaret Schink.

Sharing the work in person before the pandemic and continuing conversations and conferences via Zoom sharpened my international understanding of feminicide and genocide. The Rutgers Center for the Study of Genocide and Human Rights, Autonomous University of Chiapas, BMW Foundation and Responsible Leaders Network, Nim Ajpu La Asociación de Abogados y Notarios Mayas de Guatemala, Librería Sophos in Guatemala City, the Johannesburg Institute for Advanced Study at the University of Johannesburg in South Africa, the Association of Panzos Massacre Survivors and FAMDEGUA, the Unión Nacional de Mujeres Guatemaltecas, the Columbia Law School Society for Immigrant and Refugee Rights, the Tarrytown Jewish Community Center, the Kunst Museum of Modern Art in Frankfurt, Guelph University Community Engaged Scholarship Institute and the Department of Political Science, Leonard Lief Library at Lehman College, Harvard's Rockefeller Center for Latin American Studies, the CUNY Academy, George Mason University, Florida Gulf Coast University, Ramapo College, Programa Universitario de Estudios de Género at the Universidad Nacional Autónoma de México, Fondation Maison des sciences de l'homme in Paris, Shoah Foundation Center for Advanced Genocide Studies at the University of Southern California, University of Halle-Wittenberg, Martin Luther University, Florida Gulf Coast University, Holocaust Memorial and Tolerance Center of Nassau County, Claremont McKenna College, University of Toronto International Institute on Genocide and Human Rights, International Max Planck Research School on Retaliation, Mediation and Punishment, Halle International Policy Center, University of Michigan, Autonomous University of Madrid, Mt. Holyoke, Simmons and Smith College, Queens College, Asociación de la Mujer Guatemalteca, La Casa Encendida, and Bankia, Universidad Internacional Menéndez Pelayo, California State University Northridge and the Central American Resource Center, University of London School of Advanced Study, Teachers Union of Alta Verapaz, Facultad Latinoamericana de Ciencias Sociales, Trinity College, Univerisität Potsdam and Freie Univerisität Berlin, University of Northern British Columbia, Austrian Academy of Sciences, Inter-American Institute for Human Rights, University of Santa Clara Law, Jeju Special Self-Governing Province and the Jeju 4.3 Research Institute in South Korea, Yale University's Center on Order, Conflict and Violence, University of Oregon's Humanities Center, Kanagawa University's International Human Rights Center in Yokohama, United Nations University in Tokyo, Grinnell College, William J. Clinton Foundation, Cambridge University's McDonald Institute for Archeaological Research, Vassar College, New York University's Wagner School and Center for Latin American and Caribbean Studies, XII Salón del Libro Iberoamericano de Gijón, University of Wisconsin, New America Foundation, Strassler Center at Clark University,

Commission of Colombian Jurists, Episcopal Divinity School of Cambridge, Center for Research and Higher Study in Social Anthropology (CIESAS), Museo de Tolerancia, United States Memorial Holocaust Museum, Universidad Santo Tomas, Universidad del Rosario, Universidad Libre Los Bosques, and the National Police Academy in Bogotá provided valuable venues to exchange ideas that greatly assisted me in understanding gender violence and shaping my book.

Journalists have been important to helping me understand how to share these stories of survival and struggles for justice. Conversations with Ian Masters, Elisabeth Malkin, Julio Cisneros, Carlos Dada, Mary Louise Kelly, Cyril Mychalejko, Larry Kaplow, Alison B. Hughes, Jon Lee Anderson, Xeni Jardin, Mary Thom, Barbara Crossette, David Gonzales, Maria Martin, Miguel Ángel Albizures, Luis de León, Eduardo Barraza, and Sandra Cuffe remind me of the power of journalism and its role in democracy. I am inspired by the work of Stephen Kinzer, Alan Riding, Marlise Simons, Mary Jo McConahay, Susan Meiselas, Alicia Partnoy, Ulf Aneer, Larry Towell, Elizabeth Farnsworth, Francisco Goldman, Bill Ong Hing, Joan Kruckewitt, and Jonathan Moller.

I am immensely grateful for the close readings, support, and feedback on my final manuscript by Susan Schulman, Brigittine French, Serena Cosgrove, Jo Marie Burt, Martine Henry, Ramón González Ponciano, Ana María Méndez, Reinhard Motte, and an anonymous reviewer at the University of California Press and for the always fine editing hand of Martha Lincoln.

Researching and writing requires support on the home front from friends and family. My life is kept in balance with the unconditional love of my daughter and our extended family: Elka and John Suer, Jayme and John Daley, Martine and Adam Henry, Mildred Kilmer, Sebastian Sarti, Lauren Kawulicz, Rosario Cuevas Molina, Ana Lucía Cuevas, Heather Walsh Haney, Ken Haney, Leila, EJ,

Nana Sheila, and Vanessa and Dennis Cournoyer. The love of María Gabriela Figueroa Cuevas lives on in our hearts. My thanks to the moms (and their families) who have been my village in NYC: Jill Geisinger, Rachel Hayes, Aileen Bruner, Louise Tonkin, Sarah Nolan, Kerrie and Stephen O'Gallagher, Teia Edzgveradze, and David Kereselidze.

Last, when all is said and done, a writer needs an editor and publisher who share their vision to bring it to the public. I thank Naomi Schneider at the University of California Press for expressing early interest in my work. I especially thank my editors, Kate Marshall and Ieva Jusionyte, for their immediate and enthusiastic editorial support, as well as the UC editorial and production team: Enrique Ochoa-Kaup, Chad Attenborough, Katryce Lassle, Teresa Iafolla, Alex Dahne, Julie Van Pelt, copyeditor Sheila Berg, and indexer Thérèse Shere. Together we made this book, and it is a better book for passing through their hands. All errors are, of course, mine.

Illustrations

Abbreviations

AAAS	American Association for the Advancement of Science
AI	Amnesty International
CEH	Comisión para el Esclaramiento Histórico— Historical Clarification Commission
CIACS	Cuerpos Ilegales y Aparatos Cladestinos de Seguridad —Illegal Groups and Clandestine Security Apparatuses
CICIG	Comisión Internacional contra la Impunidad en Guatemala—International Commission against Impunity in Guatemala
CONAVIGUA	Coordinardora de las Viudas de Guatemala— Coordinating Committee of the Widows of Guatemala
DICRI	Departamento de Investigaciones Criminales— Department of Criminal Investigations
D-2	Guatemalan Ministry of Defense Intelligence; absorbed by the newly created SAAS in 2003
EAFA	Equipo de Antropología Forense de Argentina— Argentine Forensic Anthropology Team

EMP	Estado Mayor Presidencial—Presidential General Staff
EU	European Union
FAFG	Fundación de Antropología Forense de Guatemala—Guatemalan Forensic Anthropology Foundation
FAMDEGUA	Familiares de los Desaparecidos de Guatemala—Families of the Disappeared of Guatemala
GAM	Grupo de Apoyo Mutuo—Mutual Support Group
G-2	Intelligence structure of the EMP in the 1980s; became part of D-2 in 1993
IAC	Inter-American Court of Human Rights
ILO	International Labor Organization
INACIF	Instituto Nacional de Ciencias Forenses—National Institute of Forensic Sciences
INTERPOL	International Criminal Police Organization
MINUGUA	Misión de Naciones Unidas en Guatemala—United Nations Mission in Guatemala
MP	Ministerio Público—Public Ministry/Public Prosecutor's Office
PAC	Patrullas de Autodefensa Civil—Civil Defense Patrols
PAHO	Pan American Health Organization
PARLACEN	Central American Parliament
PDH	Procuraduría de Derechos Humanos—Office of the Human Rights Ombudsman
PNC	Policía Nacional Civil—National Civilian Police
OAS	Organization of American States

SAAS	Secretaría de Asuntos Administrativos y de Seguridad de la Presidencia—Secretariat of Administrative Affairs and Presidential Security
UNDP	United Nations Development Program
US CIA	United States Central Intelligence Agency
US DIA	United States Defense Intelligence Agency

Dramatis Personae

JUSTICE SEEKERS

Jorge Rolando Velásquez Durán
Esperanza (pseudonym)
Magda (pseudonym)
Maritza (pseudonym)
Lidia (pseudonym)

INTERNATIONAL INVESTIGATORS

Detective Greg Smith
Dr. Clyde Snow, Forensic Expert
Dr. Reinhard Motte, Medical Examiner
Dr. Heather Walsh Haney, Forensic Expert
Dorian Caal, Statistician

GUATEMALAN RIGHTS ADVOCATES

Amílcar Méndez
Ana María Méndez Dardón
Alba Estela Maldonado
Carolina Escobar Sarti

Carlos Pop

Norma Cruz

INTERNATIONAL HUMAN RIGHTS EXPERTS

Philip Alston, United Nations Rapporteur on Extrajudicial
Execution

Santiago Cantón, Executive Secretary, Inter-American Commission
for Human Rights

James Louis Cavallaro, Representative, Inter-American Commission for Human Rights

Yakin Ertuk, United Nations Rapporteur on Violence Against
Women

Kerry Kennedy, President, Robert F. Kennedy Foundation

Marcela Lagarde, Mexican feminist scholar

Santiago Pedraz, Judge, Spanish National Court

Iván Velásquez, Commissioner, United Nations Commission
against Impunity in Guatemala

GUATEMALAN JUSTICE OPERATORS IN
EXILE (PARTIAL LIST)

Erika Aifán, Judge

Thelma Aldana, former Attorney General

Roberto Lemus, Judge

Claudia Paz y Paz, former Attorney General

Gloria Porras, Judge

BUREAUCRATS OF IMPUNITY

Álvaro Arzú (deceased), former President of Guatemala and Mayor
of Guatemala City

Renato Durán, Prosecutor

Alejandro Giammattei, President of Guatemala and former
    Director of National Prisons
Vinicio Gómez (deceased), former Vice-Minister of the Interior
Dr. Isaias Juárez, former Director of the regional hospital in Nebaj
Álvaro Matus, Prosecutor
Otto Pérez Molina, retired General, former President indicted for
    corruption
Consuelo Porras, Attorney General
Víctor Rivera (deceased), Security Adviser
Adela Torrebiarte, former Minister of the Interior
Stefany Vásquez Barillas, Prosecutor
Carlos Vielman, former Minister of the Interior
Rodrigo Villagrán, Prosecutor

JUDGES OF THE INTER-AMERICAN COURT

Roberto F. Caldas, Brazil
Eduardo Ferrer Mac-Gregor Poisot, Mexico
Diego Garcia-Sayan, Peru
Alberto Pérez Pérez, Uruguay
Humberto Sierra Porto, Colombia
Manuel E. Ventura Robles, Costa Rica
Eduardo Vio Grossi, Chile

MAP 1. Map of Guatemala. Courtesy of F&G Editores.

Introduction

Before and After

As she drifted off to sleep, I used to tell my daughter a story about floating in the warm waves of the Pacific, the water gently lapping into a Costa Rican cove. I would describe the sun shining on us, the fresh smell of the ocean, the sweet aroma of the flowers, the salty breeze, and the sounds and colors of capuchin monkeys and toucans. Mostly, I would describe the rhythmic movement and whoosh of the water as it gently buoys your body up to the sun and back down to a new wave. And when I would give her this image to dream, I would remember the scent, sight, and sound of the ocean and tropical rain forest in Costa Rica. But that was before I began working on a Jane Doe case in Guatemala.[1] Now whenever I try to imagine water, sun, and floating, I feel that Guatemalan girl and lack sufficient imagination to visualize myself, much less my daughter, floating in the Costa Rican sun. Instead, I feel emptied by the visceral sensation of that Guatemalan girl, cold, dumped alone, lifeless, floating in dirty water on a cloudy day, waiting to be discovered in a gravel pit.

I am not the only one with a before and after on this case. Certainly, her parents have a clearly demarcated life before and after the killing of their daughter. No doubt all homicide cases carry this kind of rupture in the timeline of life for the survivors left behind. When I have worked with genocide survivors in Maya communities in Guatemala, the massacres marked their life cycles with before and after—often because they spent years in flight in the mountains after the massacres in order to survive. The Guatemalan Commission for Historical Clarification (CEH), a truth commission, documented 626 army massacres of Indigenous villages, with victims numbering more than 200,000. Among those who survived, 1.5 million were internally displaced and 150,000 sought refuge in México. While the CEH was charged with documenting the violence between 1964 and 1996, the human rights violations can be traced to the US-backed overthrow of democratically elected president Jacobo Arbenz in 1954,[2] as well as US support for army dictatorships and counterinsurgency training in the second half of the twentieth century. In international, regional, and national courts, the extreme and brutal violence of the Guatemalan army is recognized as genocide against the Maya.[3]

The violence in Guatemala was silenced for decades. The often-used terms "civil war" and "internal armed conflict" intimate some kind of parity of armed resistance and fail to capture the brutality of successive military regimes gaining and maintaining power through violence and corruption. In 1966, the Guatemalan Congress declared an army state of siege as a civil war, granting the government unlimited powers to wage war against its unarmed populace without a time limit.[4] For massacre survivors, this period is remembered as La Violencia (The Violence), and there is a before and after, not only of the massacres, but also of their lives in flight from the Guatemalan army and their return to their communities, if they returned.

The before and after of the urban experience of state terror was somewhat different because people were disappeared more often than they were openly assassinated. In fact, Guatemala is credited with having invented the political condition of being "disappeared," wherein the state or its agents detain, torture, and kill a citizen without ever acknowledging state custody of that individual. In the final four decades of the twentieth century, more people were disappeared in Guatemala than in any other Latin American country;[5] of 90,000 reported disappearances in Latin America, 50,000 happened in Guatemala, with 5,000 of those being children. For the families of the disappeared, there is only the "before." Lacking a body to bury, they are denied the closure of "after" and live in a cruel limbo of uncertainty. The ambiguity of their daily lives is reinforced by administrative denial of their condition: without a body, there is no death certificate; without a death certificate, the wife is not a widow; without the legal classification of widow, the woman cannot collect her husband's pension, claim property, or remarry.

Children of the disappeared carry the stigma of guilt by association. Though peace accords were signed and a truth commission found the Guatemalan army responsible for 93 percent of all human rights violations, the army's disinformation campaign has successfully blamed the disappeared as being responsible for their own condition, and, in fact, the army and its apologists hold the victims of the violence responsible for precipitating the army's genocide and crimes against humanity.[6]

But the Jane Doe case, like the murders of more than 500 other girls and women in 2005, happened in twenty-first-century Guatemala, nearly ten years after the 1996 peace accords were signed and more than two decades after the genocide. And, like other contemporary homicide victims, this Jane Doe was blamed for her own death.

It was in February 2007 when I first saw her in a video image taken shortly after her bloated body was found floating in shallow water in a ravine near a gravel pit on the periphery of Guatemala City. The video camera lingered over her face, which was swollen and covered with red puncture marks—marks that one US expert would later describe as probably caused by a Phillips screwdriver or knife. This day in 2007, the video of the girl was on the computer screen of a Guatemalan human rights lawyer. "The image is really harsh," she said, as she moved the screen out of sight of Jorge Velásquez, the father of Claudina Isabel, a murdered law student. "It is a girl, another feminicide case," she said. "But this one is different because powerful people are implicated."[7]

This lawyer is an important fixture in the Guatemalan human rights community. A perfectionist in every way, she sits erect, back straight, manicured and coiffed as she mulls over cases and develops legal strategies to bring perpetrators to justice. This is no small feat in a country where violence is often the first recourse for the resolution of conflict and neighbors have frequently chosen to lynch suspected criminals rather than turn them over to police. Indeed, sometimes citizens have lynched police for freeing suspected criminals. Of course, lynching victims tend to be poor and powerless. This case implicated high-ranking government officials and prominent leaders.

I agreed to the lawyer's request to look for an expert to review several cases that were far afield from my expertise at the time. There were complete copies available of several files, but this Jane Doe file lacked a duplicate. A few days later, Jorge Velásquez took me back to the Office of the Human Rights Ombudsman to pick up a complete copy of the file. After passing through several security checks and being buzzed through various doors, we were buzzed into a secure waiting room filled with a cross section of Guatemalans of all ages—rich, poor, urban, rural, white, Maya, men, women, youths—staring at the floor or whispering to their companions. Anxiety hung in the air. No one wants to be seen in the Ombudsman's Office. Fear and the need for help brought us all to this room. The receptionist called names on a microphone from behind bulletproof glass. One by one, after presenting identification again, the supplicants were buzzed in. I heard my name called over the loudspeaker, but the receptionist did not buzz me in. The lawyer I was to see was out of the office. Her secretary sent the file down with an assistant. "[NAME] CASE" was marked across the large manila envelope in thick, black letters. It made me nervous that the file was labeled with her real name because it meant that everyone who saw it (from the second-floor office down to reception and the waiting area at the Office of the Human Rights Ombudsman) would know I had the file on the extrajudicial execution of the girl. And anyone who knew what the file contained, whatever their interest might be, was surely wondering, "What is that gringa doing?" I occasionally ask myself more or less the same question. Certainly, I did not imagine that accepting the case folder meant losing a bedtime story and would eventually challenge my own sense of safety in the world.

A Cold Case

While many homicides are filed away as Jane and John Does, or in Guatemala as case XX (unidentified victims), there are also cases that should be treated as homicides but are filed away as accidents. We do not know how many of these cases exist in Guatemala. We do know that this Jane Doe case was filed away as an accident. The late, great Florida cold case detective Greg Smith told me that the girl's case should have been treated as a homicide from the moment her bloated, lifeless body was found floating in a sand pit nearly twenty miles from her home five days after she disappeared. In the United States, a case like this would be treated as a homicide until proven to be an accident.

The girl disappeared on March 5, 2005. Her dead body was found four days later. All police and morgue documents report the cadaver was in an advanced stage of decomposition. Detective Smith taught me that the first questions an investigator should ask about a dead body are, "Who is this person?" and "How did she get here?" And Detective Smith knew the questions to ask. He was the first detective in the United States dedicated to investigating cold case homicides.

But in Guatemala, the Ministerio Público (MP), or Prosecutor's Office, casts doubt on the victim and her family without ever conducting an earnest investigation. This causes Jane Doe's father to ask, "Who does the MP protect? Is the MP on the side of victims and their families or on the side of criminals? Is the prosecutor just playing with the pain of families of victims of violence in Guatemala?"

These are questions I have frequently asked myself as I investigated homicide cases in that country. I wonder how I became so deeply involved in these cases and, in the process, exposed to the intimate emotional experiences of victims and their families. While I have always found field research somewhat serendipitous, this project was like an ever-growing snowball that just dragged me along. I never sought to do this research. On the contrary, I had tried to stop working on Guatemala. In 2006, I was there simply to accompany my daughter's father and spend one semester of leave working on a book about peace communities in Colombia, but that is another story and one that is yet to be finished. I got pulled back into Guatemala when my friend Amílcar Méndez invited me to meet Jorge Velásquez, and Amílcar's daughter Ana María (whom I had known since she was three) asked me to accompany Jorge to the Prosecutor's Office as he sought justice for his daughter's murder—another young woman treated as a Jane Doe even after she was identified by her parents. Ana María went to law school with Jorge's daughter, Claudina Isabel. At the time, I was confused about what they wanted me to do. My previous work in Guatemala had been mainly with Maya massacre survivors in rural communities, which is how I met Amílcar, who was honored in the 1980s with Kennedy, Carter, and Mitterand awards for his brave human rights work with K'iche' Maya communities.[8] In the process of my research on genocide, I had worked on an exhumation in Amílcar's home community of San Andrés Sajcabajá and accompanied the mostly monolingual K'iche' Maya–language speakers as they sought justice from a nonresponsive legal system. Now Amílcar and Ana María were asking me to accompany Jorge, a sophisticated, urbane, conservative, evangelical, upper-middle-class auditor who is taller than me and whiter than me. I did not understand why Jorge needed me to accompany him. After all, his Spanish is better than mine.

Against my better judgment, I agreed to accompany Jorge because of my profound respect for Amílcar, who at the height of the genocide had collected more than thirteen thousand thumbprint signatures from illiterate Maya peasants who did not want to participate in compulsory army-controlled civil patrols. I also appreciated the earnest efforts of 19-year-old Ana María trying to unravel the murder of her friend during her first year of law school. Now an international human rights lawyer, Ana María remembers her decision to seek justice for Claudina Isabel: "I could not stand by without doing something. In my family, we were taught to struggle for justice regardless of the cost—to defend life and practice solidarity."[9] Ana María began to accompany Jorge and introduced him to her father, insisting that they had the right to demand the truth of what happened to Claudina Isabel and that her murder should be investigated and the perpetrators brought to justice. Then they reached out to me.

For my part, I acquiesced to the accompaniment because I was guessing that Jorge and I would not get along alone for more than about fifteen minutes: I mistakenly expected him to try to evangelize me. He never has, and all these years later, I continue to accompany him and his family as they seek justice for his daughter's murder.

Perhaps this is one of the backstories of this story. It is also my account of how I, a mostly left-leaning, not very orthodox feminist, California native turned New Yorker, and new mother late in life, found myself working for justice in Guatemala with an evangelical auditor, a cold case detective, and Florida forensic experts.

Crime Scene Photos from *Killer's Paradise*

I remember back in 2006. After one of our meetings, my daughter and I are walking Jorge Velásquez to his car.[10] I am recounting her storytelling to dinner guests the night before: "Jorge lifts me up. He can hold me high." He laughs and effortlessly lifts her to touch a peeling poster two meters above on a lamppost and flowers high up in a tree, both far beyond my reach. She has just recently turned two. He smiles and shakes his head as he says what I had already imagined: "She reminds me . . . I remember Claudina Isabel. The memories are bittersweet. I remember her exploring the world and touching new things. And then it is over. Only God knows why." He passes my daughter back as he gives me an envelope sealed and wrapped tightly with tape.

Later I take the envelope to a graphic designer friend who has agreed to scan the contents. When I hand him the sealed envelope, he looks at me quizzically as he asks about the sizes of the images. I tell him, "I haven't found the courage to look at them. I don't know their size. I don't even know if they are useful." Jorge had never looked at these images either. Inside the envelope are crime scene photos from his daughter Claudina Isabel's murder. These photos are the first official documentation of her death and the only photos available for forensic analysis. I need scans of the images to send to forensic anthropologists, cold case detectives, and medical examiners who are willing to donate their time and skills to offer an expert opinion on the case (and later become part of my team).

FIGURE 1. Photo of Claudina Isabel Velásquez Paiz at University of San Carlos Law School. Courtesy of Ana María Méndez Dardón.

Jorge told me he can only look at photos of Claudina Isabel when he is with friends or when he must do so in a public presentation. But he is referring to photos of his daughter when she was alive. Sometimes he will ask me, "She was beautiful my little girl, wasn't she?" The truth is that she was a stunning young woman. I have only seen her in photos and family videos. In these images, she fills whatever space she occupies with life. Her smile is lovely and inviting. She is happy and engaged with the world. This is how I see her through her father's eyes and in the photos he has shared with me.

My friend brings the scans to my house. He tells me the photos are small. They should have been larger; we had expected 8 × 10s. He has scanned them and labeled them. He gives me the CD-ROMs to send to experts who know how to interpret this material. I know she was killed. I know she was beaten. I believe she was raped. I know she took a bullet through her forehead. I know she had an injury over one of her eyes that looked like it came from a glass or a bottle or a pipe. I know her clothes were in disarray. Her belt was undone. Her sweater was on backward, and her pant zipper was down. I know all this from reading incomplete forensic reports, analyses of incomplete forensic reports, and discussions with lawyers and others with no forensic training trying to understand the case.

I prepare the packages to send to the forensic anthropologists— one in New York, one in Florida, and one in London. I receive a call from Jorge, and we discuss a meeting we will have the next morning. I tell him the scans are done. We agree he will retrieve the originals when we meet in order to return them to their source. As we say good-bye, he says, "It is tempting to look at them, no?" Not a challenge, not quite a request, but a tepid invitation, because Jorge would never ask me to do something he did not feel comfortable doing himself.

After I hang up the phone, I summon my courage, the adrenaline runs through my arms and to my stomach, making me feel a bit nau-seated. I open the envelope. The first photos are taken from a dis-tance. She is lying in the gutter of a trash-strewn street, half on the sidewalk. Someone has covered her with a white sheet. Who did this? Her tormentor? The person who called the fire department?

I move on to the next photo. The sheet is removed. Her body is twisted, her hand almost pointing at something above her. It looks like she is turning to say something, which she is not, because her face is directly in the gutter. Now I see the open belt and zipper. I see the curve of her waist, her smooth, milky skin, her bare belly with a little ring in the belly button. Her body still looks alive. I see her san-dals and her pink sweater.

I turn the page. Her head has been moved. Her face is covered with a splash of blood from the bullet that went through her fore-head. I can't look at the photo long enough to consider the injury to her eye. I notice her mouth is swollen, her lip is split, a dark thread of blood runs from her nose.

I move to the next photo. I see a close-up of the bullet entry wound in her forehead. I see gloved hands with blood-covered fingers manipulating her head to measure the exit wound with a ruler. Her hair is matted with blood. I am unable to look at the measurement. The blood-covered fingers are too much for me.

Then her sweater is off and spread out in the street. What? I check back to the first photos. She was wearing the sweater. Why did they remove it in the street? Now they have left her near-naked upper body lying directly on the bloody pavement. And then I notice there is not very much blood around her given how bloody her head and face seem to be. But I stop looking. It is too much. Still, I almost can't stop myself from calling Jorge to ask him if he knew they removed her sweater at the crime scene. I stop myself. He doesn't need to imagine this at night. And with profound sadness, I realize that sooner or later, Jorge will have to look at these photos of his beloved Claudina Isabel dead in the street. And I cry.[11]

The Killing of Women in Guatemala

Claudina Isabel and Jane Doe were among the 518 women and girls who were murdered in 2005 alone. Most of the women killed were between 16 and 30 years old. In 2005, Jane Doe was one of the 68 girl murder victims under the age of 17.[12] With each year that passes, it becomes ever more dangerous to be female in Guatemala. More than 600 women were killed in 2006. Since the murders of Claudina Isabel and Jane Doe in 2005, on average, two Guatemalan women have been murdered each day.[13] Indeed, the mortality rate of women in peacetime Guatemala today is approaching the very high levels of female mortality recorded in the early 1980s, at the height of the genocidal war that ultimately claimed the lives of 200,000 men, women, and children.[14]

The intensity of violence in Guatemala is as high as it was during the war. More than 600 women were killed in 1982 at the height of the genocide, and ten years after the murder of Claudina Isabel, more than 600 women were killed in "peacetime" Guatemala in 2015. The danger is real, and my research indicates that the most dangerous places in Guatemala are private spaces and frontiers between rural and urban communities, between marginalized urban barrios and established commercial centers—all frontiers that need to be crossed by women in pursuit of education, employment, and the reproduction of daily life.

The Pan-American Health Organization (PAHO) classifies more than 10 homicides per 100,000 inhabitants as an epidemic and a public health concern. In 2005, there were 42 homicides for every 100,000 inhabitants in Guatemala—ten times the murder rate in New York.[15] In Japan, there was less than 1 murder per 100,000 inhabitants;[16] in the United States, the murder rate was roughly 9.8 per 100,000, the same rate since 1980;[17] Venezuela's homicide rate was 33 per 100,000; and Mexico had a rate of 19 per 100,000 in 2013.[18] In Latin America, the average number of murders for each 100,000 inhabitants was 30.[19]

Between 2002 and 2005, there were 1,715 female homicides and 15,998 male homicides in Guatemala—a national total of 17,713 people killed in four years.[20] Between 2002 and 2005, the number of women killed increased by more than 63 percent, and nearly 40 percent of these murders—or at least the murders that were reported—happened in or near Guatemala City. Boys and young men are at risk of homicide from gangs and paramilitary groups. Girls and women are at risk of rape, torture, and homicide from gangs and paramilitary groups, as well as gender-based violence in their homes and communities. UNICEF estimates that sexual abuse affects 1 of 4 girls and 18 percent of boys in Guatemala.[21] This high level of violence is paralyzing in daily life.

Guatemalan women as a group are subject to danger, violence, and oppression simply because they are women. Patriarchy, misogyny, and inequality structure women's lives. Their gender makes them a target, deprives them of security and protection, and limits their freedom in all aspects of their lives. During the pandemic lockdown from March to June 2020, at least 140 women were killed, more than 19,000 women reported incidents of violence to the Ministerio Público, and 403 emergency alerts were issued for missing women.[22] In the first eight months of 2021, Guatemala registered a 31 percent increase in the murder of women, and 58,975 crimes against women and children were registered by the Women's Observatory of the MP. Mario Polanco, director of the Mutual Support Group, explained that the increase in crimes of violence against women is directly related to the lack of attention authorities give to women reporting threats of violence and intimidation that ultimately lead to homicide.[23]

Gender Violence and Feminicide

It is in the ambience of gender violence that two Guatemalan women lose their lives each day. The combination of impunity and gender-based discrimination grounded in patriarchy is among the factors that nurture a culture of violence in which men, whether spouses or security forces, believe that women are their property to do with as they wish. If a woman is living with an abusive man, no one dares to intervene and offend that man's honor. If that woman flees the abuse, in the same man's absence she has no one to defend her honor or signal to security forces that she is not somehow suspect. This means that young, single women and women fleeing violent relationships are in an extraordinarily weak societal position when confronted with the harassment and violence of men, and they are especially vulnerable to the whims of security forces and gangs.

At the same time, the Guatemalan State has failed to create juridical and social conditions to ensure the safety and security of female members of the society. Amnesty International concluded that the very way in which the Guatemalan government classifies causes of death in homicide statistics unnecessarily complicates the little information available and hides "the brutality based on gender and the sexual nature of many of these crimes."[24] UN reports have also pointed out that intersecting systems of inequality and gender hierarchies create layers of discrimination and exclusion for different groups of women in Guatemala and that women's exposure to violence is related to their position within these systems of exclusion.[25]

In this book, I use the term "feminicide" to discuss the killing of women in Guatemala. "Feminicide" refers to the murder of women by men because they are women and also points to state responsibility for these murders whether through commission of the actual killing, toleration of the perpetrators' acts of violence, or omission of State responsibility to ensure the safety of its female citizens. As Marcela Lagarde has noted in her work on feminicide in Ciudad Juárez, Mexico, "Feminicide occurs when the authorities fail to efficiently carry out their duties to prevent and punish [the killing of women] and thus create an environment of impunity."[26] Indeed, feminicide in Latin America first came to international attention with the killings of young women in Ciudad Juárez in the early 1990s. While there are similarities in the patterns of registered murders of women in Ciudad Juárez and Guatemala, the murder rate of women in Guatemala is much higher. Between 1993 and 2003, there were 370 registered murders of women in the Mexican state of Chihuahua in which Ciudad Juárez is located.[27] In just one year, 2003, there were 383 registered murders of women in Guatemala, and that number would soon double.[28]

Feminicide's death toll is the most horrifying quantification of these fundamentally unacceptable attitudes and structures, but it is far from the whole problem. The cost of these killings in lost lives and lost futures is brutal. As UN Rapporteur on Extrajudicial Execution Philip Alston notes, "The death toll is only the beginning of the cost, for a society that lives in fear of killing is unable to get on with its life and business in the ways that it wants." Moreover, Alston points out that while the female population increased by 8 percent between 2001 and 2006, the female homicide rate increased by more than 117 percent.[29] In *Textures of Terror*, I explore the costs of these murders for individuals, families, and Guatemalan society by investigating the case of Claudina Isabel and others in the wider context of gender violence in its multiple forms.

Claudina Isabel's murder and the efforts of her father to bring her murderer(s) to justice not only provide a lens into the suffering and loss of an affected family but also offer an up-close appraisal of the inner workings of the Guatemalan criminal justice system and its role in the maintenance of inequality, patriarchy, power, and impunity. This book is about women, violence, and migration coming out of Guatemala and the US role in this violence from the genocide of the 1980s to the present. As we come to terms with histories of carceral regimes in the United States and the violence meted out against Indigenous women and their ongoing disappearance in the United States,[30] it is worth noting that the Florence, Arizona, Detention Center used today to detain and process refugees was originally established as a POW camp in 1942 to hold captured Italians, Germans, and Austrians. The camp was transformed into a detention center for the illegal internment of American citizens of Japanese ancestry under the War Relocation Act in 1943. Dylan S. Myer, the presidentially appointed intellectual author of the Japanese internment camps, next took his carceral experience to the Bureau of Indian Affairs, which runs Native American reservations.[31] As you read this book, Central American refugees are being detained in and deported from this prison in Florence, Arizona.

This book is about confronting impunity while living on the uncertain and hazy frontiers of life and death. It is about my contact with the private traumas of others as they face terror, as well as their own haunting feelings of inadequacy in the midst of unimaginable levels of violence. It is about the unreliability of memory and the slipperiness of truth as each are deployed to counter silence and demand justice for unspeakable crimes. It is my journey through memory, violence, and recovery in Guatemala. The story of Jorge Velásquez's quest for justice for the murder of his daughter and the stories of other women seeking help or safe haven from crime and terror simultaneously transcend the individual and teach us all something about humanity and ourselves.

Throughout the book, I weave vignettes from my forensic experiences investigating the genocide into my current work on cases of feminicide, extrajudicial execution, and social cleansing. I highlight the ways military structures of the past have morphed into and overlap with contemporary structures of violence: gangs, drug traffickers, and organized crime. The ripple effects of violence, as well as corruption, in Guatemala are seen in the plight of refugees at our southern border and Guatemalan justice operators seeking political asylum in the United States. These transitions of violence and corruption have devastating consequences for all Guatemalans but especially Guatemalan women. This book provides a framework for understanding why and how Guatemalan men, women, youths, and children are fleeing criminal violence in all its public and private manifestations. The survivor experiences of domestic violence show the links to larger histories of public and private violence, as well as the institutional exclusion of Indigenous communities and the intersectionality of these histories of exclusion with the second-class status of women and girls.

1   *The Night Claudina Isabel Did Not Come Home*

The last time Claudina Isabel communicated with her parents was around 11:45 p.m. on August 12, 2005.[1] Around two in the morning on August 13 her parents were awakened by Zully Moreno, the mother of Claudina Isabel's boyfriend, Pedro Samayoa Moreno, who went to their home to inform them that Claudina Isabel was in grave danger. Señora Moreno claimed that Claudina Isabel called her to tell her she was walking home and that this call was cut short by Claudina Isabel's screams for help. Claudina Isabel's parents immediately went out to search for their daughter—first at the house where Claudina Isabel had attended a party in the nearby middle-class neighborhood of Colonia Panorama. With no results or leads from the partygoers, they began to search the neighborhoods from the party back to their home.

Desperate, they attempted to make a report at the local police station at about 3:00 a.m. on August 13. The police, however, refused to take a report or even listen to the worried parents. They suggested that Claudina Isabel had run off with her boyfriend and that, in any case, they would not receive any reports until Claudina Isabel had been officially missing for twenty-four hours. It was not until 8:30 in the morning that the police formally received Claudina Isabel's parents and made an official report that classified Claudina Isabel

Velásquez Paiz as missing. This was three and one-half hours after her lifeless body was found in the street on 10th Avenue in Colonia Roosevelt in Zone 11—a neighborhood not more than two miles from the party where she was last seen by friends. Despite the obvious connection between the location of Claudina Isabel's body and her parents' anguished report to the police, she was not identified until much later that day and only then because of her parents' efforts to locate her.

In fact, Claudina Isabel's case, like Jane Doe's and the other 516 murder cases of women in Guatemala in 2005, was dismissed from the moment her cadaver was found. This was because, as one official acknowledged, "the crime scene was not developed as it should have been because of prejudices about the social origin and status of the victim. She was classified as a person whose death did not merit investigation."[2] The first police officers on the scene determined that Claudina Isabel's murder was "not worthy" of investigation because she had a belly button ring and was wearing sandals. In the eyes of the Guatemalan police, this meant she was a gang member or a prostitute.

But Claudina Isabel was not a gang member or a prostitute. Claudina Isabel Velásquez Paiz was a 19-year-old law student, beautiful, gregarious, and well liked by her peers. More than a thousand people attended her memorial service. Ana María Méndez was among the many law students in attendance. "We were young women of 19, beginning our lives, chasing our dreams," she remembers. "We were defining ourselves as women—an act of self-determination. In 2005, we didn't really speak of feminism, but somehow Claudina and my other friends, we were living it because nothing stopped us." The murder of Claudina Isabel forever changed the lives of these young female law students. "Everything collapsed," explained Ana María. "The bright paths we imagined were darkened and cut short with death. I studied law, I believed in justice, and I simply could not understand why they had erased Claudina's smile from our lives."[3]

At the memorial service, Jorge Velásquez did not understand what was happening when several armed police officers in uniforms with vests marked "Policía" arrived and demanded access to his daughter's body. When Jorge refused, the police threatened to arrest him and his wife. The coffin was removed from the memorial service and placed in a private room where police officers unceremoniously took fingerprints and nail clippings from the cadaver in the coffin. When they were finished collecting this material for forensic analysis, they handed Jorge a paper bag. In response to his dismay, the officer explained that the bag contained the clothing Claudina Isabel had been wearing at the time she was murdered. "Most families bury the clothing in the coffin," the police said matter-of-factly. Distraught, Jorge responded that he would not be burying the clothing in a coffin, that he would not allow them to ever again disturb his daughter. Without thinking about the implications, he asked the funeral home to burn the bag and its contents—which in murder cases throughout most of the world would have been part of the evidence held on file by investigators.

Jorge remembers the memorial service: "Claudina Isabel was so loved by everyone. There were a thousand people at her memorial service. We were so moved by her friends, students from the university. They spoke so highly of her. They loved her. It was oddly satisfying. There is a kind of adrenaline that sets in and moves you through disaster. The memorial service, in spite of the police disrupting everything, was profoundly moving. We were near euphoric. Then, when it was over, we got home and reality knocked us down. The euphoria evaporated. She was gone. She was dead. We would never see her again." And he breaks down in sobs.

I have learned all this and more about the case of Claudina Isabel Velásquez Paiz—first, from a 2006 BBC documentary, *Killer's*

Paradise, about the feminicide in Guatemala. The first time I heard the film, I was sitting in a room adjacent to where it was being screened. I was nursing my daughter as she fell asleep in my arms. I did not want to expose her, even in infancy, to this violence that is so penetrating of the heart and spirit. I wanted to spare her from the "susto" that so many Guatemalans suffer and sometimes die from. *Susto* means "fright," but in Guatemala it means much more. In Western parlance, the survivors are suffering from post-traumatic stress disorder (PTSD). But susto is something more, a malady of the soul and spirit. I learned about susto when I was working with Maya massacre survivors in the mountains. In Guatemala, Indigenous women believe they pass their sorrows and fear to their children through their breast milk; recent Western medicine research on the relationship between stress and breast milk composition supports this Maya belief.[4]

And I have learned even more following Claudina Isabel's case since July 2006, accompanying Jorge in his search for justice, and conducting my own research on the killing of women in Guatemala. Amílcar Méndez first showed me the film in 2006 when he and Ana María introduced me to Jorge. Human rights plaques and trophies from the Robert F. Kennedy Foundation, the Carter Center for Human Rights, and the Mitterand Award for Human Rights compete with family photos for shelf space in the spartan living room of the Méndez family. It was there that Amílcar also showed me a collection of daily clippings of images of murdered young women from Guatemalan newspapers. He showed me a video montage he had made of television news footage that shows the cadavers of young men and women casually thrown into the back of police trucks every day. He explained to me that Jorge needed accompaniment for the same reasons that Maya communities needed accompaniment—to not be alone confronting the legal system and to have a witness to his struggle for justice. Thus began my journey through the land of pale hands—

Guatemala in the twenty-first century, some twenty-five years after the genocide that took the lives of 200,000 Guatemalans—a journey through unchecked impunity more than two decades after the Peace Accords and a truth commission.

As I watched the early twenty-first-century footage of human bodies being tossed into trucks like bags of garbage and tried to block out the sharp and heavy thuds of the elbows, knees, and heads slamming unceremoniously on the truck beds, I wondered about the source of this kind of violence and the casually cruel disregard for humanity, from the killer to those throwing the bodies in the truck to the film crews recording it every night. Is this what happens when the intellectual authors of genocide and their agents of death are not brought to justice? Is it even possible for past and present violence to not be related? If I assume that feminicide, the killing of women, is nurtured by the same structures of terror that generated genocide, who is being killed? And who is doing the killing? In this book, I explore these questions as I accompany Jorge and work with human rights advocates, forensic experts, and crime scene investigators on specific cases of gender violence and feminicide.

Crime Scene Investigation

There are no binding international standards for murder investigations, but basic investigative procedures vary little internationally, and nowhere is it suggested as a good investigative procedure to return the clothing of a murder victim to the family for burial with the body. In fact, if there is anything remarkable about standard protocols, it is their procedural simplicity and scientific consistency regardless of the complexity of the case. The first task is to secure the crime scene and document all the evidence by mapping, photographing, and collecting everything possible, from bloodstains to footprints. The body should then be removed from the scene and taken to the morgue for a complete medico-legal autopsy. This should include examination of all internal organs, including the brain. Samples of blood and possibly other fluids should be taken for toxicology examination to review for the presence of drugs, alcohol, or other toxic agents. If sexual assault is suspected, vaginal, rectal, and oral swabs should be taken to collect seminal fluids for DNA analysis. It is during this autopsy that fingernail scrapings and finger-prints should also be collected for DNA studies. In cases with gun-shot wounds or blunt force traumas, radiographs should also be taken.

Prior to the autopsy, the clothing is removed from the victim. This is usually done with pinking shears to avoid any confusion with tears to the clothing that may have been caused by knives, bullets, or strug-gles during the assault. Hair and other fibers on the clothing (and body) should also be collected for microscopic examination. Any stains caused by blood or other bodily fluid would also be collected from the clothing. Any tears in the clothing are studied to determine their size, pattern, and relation to the wounds the victim suffered. After all this review of the clothing is completed, it is retained as evi-dence. The legendary forensic anthropologist Dr. Clyde Snow told me that the victim's clothing is not returned to the next of kin. Per-sonal effects, such as jewelry or other valuables, may be returned to the family provided they do not have evidentiary value. If retained as evidence, they are not returned to the family until after the trial.[5] This, of course, assumes there will be a trial, which assumes there will be an arrest, which assumes there will be an investigation that leads to a suspect.

At 5:30 in the morning of August 13 when an anonymous call was made to the fire station to report a body in the street on 10th Avenue, Claudina Isabel's parents were still searching for her and trying to enlist local police in their efforts. Mr. and Mrs. Velásquez went to the homes of their daughter's friends hoping to find her there. They then began to search for her at hospitals and morgues. At noon on August 13, Mrs. Velásquez identified the lifeless, bruised body of her daughter at the morgue. What happened to Claudina Isabel? What were the circumstances of her death? Who killed her? Where? How? These are questions that should have driven an investigation of her murder. More than a decade after Claudina Isabel's murder, her parents, family, and friends continue to ask these questions. In 2005, her father also began to ask what happened to his daughter's body after it was found by the authorities. What were the investigative procedures that were followed?

Jorge Velásquez is 63 years old. He is tall and trim and wears conservative business suits—usually pinstriped and always with a tie. With his short-trimmed gray hair, blue eyes, and soft-spoken yet confident demeanor, one can imagine him patiently explaining an audit to a client. Jorge is an accountant by training, but since September 2005, instead of auditing companies for a living, he has dedicated his life to seeking a resolution for his daughter's murder. Perhaps without meaning to do so, perhaps because it is simply the framework within which his accountant's mind processes the debits and credits of life, Jorge has effectively audited the judicial system's response to his daughter's murder. The results of this audit offer us the most comprehensive assessment available of the Guatemalan justice system and its bankrupt response to crime victims seeking justice.

From Crime Scene to Forensic Investigation

In Guatemala, the first to arrive at the scene of a crime are the local volunteer firefighters. Paramedics may arrive as well. The firefighters then notify the police, who are charged with securing and investigating the crime scene—the site where the body is found. The firefighters also notify the MP investigative unit, the Department of Criminal Investigations (DICRI), which is also charged with securing and investigating the crime scene. DICRI used to include a forensic doctor, but somewhat inexplicably, it no longer does. After the crime scene investigation is complete and the competing investigative units from the police and MP have thoroughly tromped all over the crime scene, the cadaver is transferred to the morgue, where a forensic doctor, or a physician who claims to be a forensic doctor, will carry out an autopsy—sometimes thorough, sometimes not.

Today the Instituto Nacional de Ciencias Forenses de Guatemala (INACIF; National Institute of Forensic Science of Guatemala), the national morgue, carries out the autopsies. INACIF did not exist when Claudina Isabel was murdered. Claudina Isabel's body was taken to the city morgue, where a forensic doctor of the Organismo Judicial (court system) carried out the autopsy. In Guatemala, those performing autopsies often have no formal training in forensics. Thus the designation "forensic doctor" is truly in name only. And those who are forensic doctors at INACIF are extremely distrustful of outside experts and at the same time seek approbation from highly trained international experts. On one occasion during an autopsy carried out by my team in Guatemala, our forensic doctor, who is a county medical examiner at a large metropolitan morgue, was subjected to a rudimentary anatomy lesson by the INACIF forensic doctor assigned to the case. This slowed the autopsy and was distracting, but we feared any effort to stop his diatribe might interfere with our ability to continue the autopsy because the INACIF forensic doctor is required to be present. Because we worked as a team, our goal was always to do whatever was necessary to complete our job.

Ideally, police and prosecution investigators would work together with the medical examiner to collect as much information as possible with the goal of solving the crime. Unfortunately, the norm in Guatemalan investigations is the opposite of team collaboration. Though INACIF was established in 2007 to professionalize and improve Guatemalan forensic capabilities, many human rights advocates find that INACIF is a gatekeeper of the justice system rather than an investigative unit gathering evidence for homicide prosecutions.

Many Guatemalan citizens do not seek police protection for fear of police complicity or retaliation from gangs or organized crime if they attempt to make a report. Sometimes the line between perpetrator culpability and state complicity is not clear. For example, in 2013, eight police officers were killed in the Salcajá police station in Quetzaltenango. It was initially believed that the police were killed by a local kingpin drug trafficker, Guayo Cano, in retaliation for having detained several of his armed bodyguards earlier that week.[6] In 2015, it came out that the 2013 killings were revenge against the police chief, who was kidnapped and burned to death by Cano's henchmen, under his order, as punishment for stealing $740,000 from Cano's organization. Cano's operation involved more than twenty of his henchmen and included an informant from INACIF who advised Cano that INACIF had the burned remains of the police chief.[7] Cano was the Mexican Cartel del Golfo's top capo in Guatemala; he was apprehended in Tuxtla Gutiérrez, Mexico, in 2018 and remanded to Guatemala for trial.[8] Six months later, he was sentenced to 372 years in prison for the massacre of police officers.[9] When citizens do make complaints, they know they are entering the murky structural corruption of police, drug traffickers, and INACIF.

But keeping the focus on Claudina Isabel, there are many unexplained incidents in her case, beginning with the crime scene. Claudina Isabel was covered with a sheet before the crime scene investigation began. Where did the sheet come from? Who covered her? These are logical questions. Minimally, the presence of the sheet indicates that someone had access to her cadaver before the authorities. While the sheet is present in the first crime scene photos, it was neither kept nor examined as evidence. There is no record of the names of the paramedics who were the first on the scene, which means there is no record of whatever types of manipulations they may have done to her body to either attempt to resuscitate her or determine that she was dead. It is also unclear how long the crime scene investigation lasted. The MP auxiliary investigator claims they spent one hour, from 6:30 to 7:30 a.m., documenting the crime scene and collecting evidence. The prosecutor's medical examiner states in his autopsy report that he completed the autopsy at 8:10 a.m. The morgue register indicates that the cadaver was received at 6:30 a.m. There is no clear inventory of the victim's clothing, nor is there any clarity as to whether any forensic examination of her clothing was actually conducted. And the police report, which is dated August 16, 2005,[10] casts doubt on its contents by failing to note that Claudina Isabel's fingerprints and fingernail shavings were taken at the funeral home during a public memorial service, not during the crime scene investigation or during the autopsy three days earlier, on August 13, 2005.

Although Claudina Isabel's body was found in front of a house that also has an informal restaurant, no effort was made by either the police or the prosecution investigators to search the house or restaurant for bloodstains or other evidence. Likewise, it is unclear if the inhabitants of the house were ever interviewed because witnesses were not identified and no follow-up interviews were conducted. The report states that various witnesses (whose names are not provided) saw a vehicle that resembled a white taxi at the crime scene. Both the prosecutor and police reports cite these witnesses as "witnesses who prefer not to be identified."[11] While both the prosecutor and the police carried out interviews, these were conducted separately, and there were no efforts made by the different investigators to meet or compare notes to develop lines of investigation.

There is tremendous confusion about the most basic and critical pieces of forensic information, such as the time of death. The medical examiner states in his report that death occurred between "one and three hours" but does not indicate whether he is referring to between one and three in the morning or between one and three hours before the autopsy. Whatever the case may be, given that the autopsy was completed at 8:10 a.m. according to the medical examiner, it is unclear whether between "one and three hours" refers to the actual autopsy or when the cadaver was first examined on the scene at 6:30 a.m. In addition, neither the body temperature of the victim nor the ambient temperature is included in the report—both of which are critical for determining approximate time of death.

Significant discrepancies in the identification of actual injuries sustained by Claudina Isabel appear among the various reports. The MP report does not include injuries that are visible in the crime scene photos and are also described in the police report, which includes reference to significant bruising to the left eye socket and cheek. The medical examiner also fails to note severe scraping on the left knee and right flank—both of which also appear in the photos and are mentioned in the police report as well. There is no documentation indicating the sampling or analysis of bloodstains—neither from the victim's clothing nor at the crime scene. While the medical examiner indicates that there was some kind of postmortem manipulation of the cadaver, there is no explanation of what this might have entailed or its significance to the case.

The official autopsy report indicates that various pieces of clothing had bloodstains, that the victim's bra and belt had been removed, and that her pants zipper was down and her blouse was on backward. Only her blouse was submitted for analysis; no analysis was done on the rest of her clothing. And there is no indication in the report that any effort was made to collect fingerprints from the blouse. Claudina Isabel sustained a gunshot wound to the head, and there is a photo of a gloved hand holding a ruler and manipulating the head, but there is no indication in the report about the angle or pathway of the bullet, which could indicate the position of the victim and the murderer when the gun was fired. There is also no indication as to whether the location where Claudina Isabel's body was found is the location where she was killed—another critical piece of information in a murder investigation. The lack of a blood pool near her body casts doubt that the location where she was found is the location where she was killed. While the crime scene investigation was completed by 7:30 a.m. on August 13, the report of the medical examiner from the crime scene was not written until seventeen days later, August 30, 2005, and it took until November 2005 for it to be incorporated into the investigation file at the MP.[12] So the prosecutors charged with investigating Claudina Isabel's murder did not have access to the report of the medical examiner until three months after her death.

Likewise, the autopsy conducted at the morgue is full of omissions and inconsistencies, beginning with who actually carried out the autopsy because the medical examiner does not list the names of those who participated—which is standard practice. It took the medical examiner more than a year to report the time of death and nearly two months to include Claudina Isabel's name on the report. The initial report states that an autopsy was carried out on a female person identified as "XX" of approximately 20 years of age at 11:00 a.m. on August 13, 2005. Although this report carries a date of August 16, 2005, and Claudina Isabel's mother identified her body at noon on August 13, the medical examiner never added Claudina Isabel's name to the report. This omission had to be corrected officially following a formal request from the MP (which was only made at the insistence of Mr. Velásquez—and this correction was not made until October 7, 2005). In the same official correction adding Claudina Isabel's name, the medical examiner clarified the confusion over the time of death. Rather than between "one and three hours," the medical examiner wrote on October 7 that "the time of death was between seven and eleven hours *after* the autopsy" (my emphasis)—

which would mean that Claudina Isabel was alive at the time of the autopsy. It was not until June 7, 2006, that the medical examiner corrected this error and indicated that the time of death was between seven and eleven hours before the autopsy. And in this report, nearly one year after Claudina Isabel's death and even though her name was now on the file, the medical examiner still refers to her as an unknown "XX."

The failure to record the name of the victim on her file after she is identified, the bureaucratic lag time and administrative obstacles to get her name on the file, and the negation of Claudina Isabel's individual dignity by choosing to name her "XX" raise a number of troubling issues. Refusing to name Claudina Isabel is a form of administrative erasure of her humanity and right to dignity. Every time a woman is murdered and "XX" is placed on her file instead of her name, the state participates in the invisibilization of violence against women by othering feminicide victims into namelessness. Naming Claudina Isabel's file "XX" even though she was already identified casts doubt on police, INACIF, and Prosecutor's Office statements that no one claims the bodies of the "XX" female victims. It also puts into question all aspects of the investigation of every feminicide case labeled "XX."

In Claudina Isabel's case, no bullet pathway and no angle have ever been attributed to the bullet wound to her head. Contusions and bruises on her eye and jaw have never been included or analyzed in any forensic report. In addition, a significant hemorrhage near her nose is obvious in photos and video taken at the crime scene but absent from the forensic report. Likewise, the omission of the severe scrapes to her left knee, right flank, and toes of the left foot leaves as a permanent point of speculation whether these injuries were sustained during a struggle or were postmortem injuries sustained while Claudina Isabel's body was moved from wherever she was killed to where her body was discovered.

Dr. Reinhard Motte, retired associate medical examiner for Palm Beach County, tells me that differentiation of pre- and postmortem trauma is important. If a living person suffers a trauma premortem, swelling (edema) and bruising (contusion) will follow. This is why when you bang your leg on the corner of a coffee table, you end up with a bruised lump. Dr. Motte explains that in a living person, "the swelling is caused by capillaries becoming leaky, allowing fluid from blood to leak into tissue to begin the healing process."

Capillaries are the smallest blood vessels in our bodies. They are located in the tissue and organs and play an important role in micro-circulation of blood from the heart through a complex system of veins, arteries, venules, and capillaries. Arteries move blood from the heart and veins move it back to the heart. Capillaries move blood from arteries to veins. Greater trauma means more small blood vessels, like capillaries, are torn, which, in turn, means that blood is pumped into surrounding tissue causing bruising.

"A dead person shows no tissue reaction," explains Dr. Motte. "Contusions are absent. Bone fractures will not have associated contusion because the heart is not beating and not pumping blood into the surrounding damaged tissue. Abrasions (scrapes) and lacerations (tearing) will look plain, with no swelling or bleeding."

When a living person scrapes her knee or elbow, the skin surface will be red because of the blood pumping through her body. If a dead person's body is scraped, the skin will appear yellow, rather than red, because the heart is no longer pumping blood. While there are some exceptions to the rule (and a trained pathologist can identify them), the bottom line here is that trauma injuries to a living person look different from those that occurred after death. As Dr. Motte summed it up, "Next time you are in a butcher shop, note the lack of bruising on the meat. This is because animals are butchered when dead. Or cut into a steak, and you will see no bruising, and you can think of me."

While gallows humor helps those on the front lines make it through their work, these are important distinctions. The police report noted significant bruising on the left eye socket and cheek as well as scraping on the left knee and flank. These abrasions and contusions are also visible in the crime scene photos. Minimally, this indicates that the bruises and abrasions happened to Claudina Isabel's body before the police were on the scene, which also means that these particular injuries did not happen while transporting the body to the morgue. However, it does not tell us whether these injuries are pre- or postmortem. A thorough analysis of these injuries by the medical examiner could have helped the investigation significantly. For example, if the medical examiner determined that these were postmortem injuries, this would lead to investigating where and how these after-death injuries occurred. Postmortem injuries could indicate that her body was moved from the original crime scene (where she was killed) to the secondary crime scene (where her body was discovered). In the absence of a medical analysis of these bruises and contusions, the medical examiner's observation about postmortem manipulation of the cadaver leaves us hanging. Did this postmortem manipulation happen when Claudina Isabel's body was moved from the street to the morgue transport vehicle (which was most likely the back of a pickup truck), from the transport vehicle to the morgue waiting area, from the waiting area to the examining table? Or did the medical examiner see something that indicated crime scene manipulation but fail to mention it?

Dr. Motte explained that a thorough analysis of contusions is very important to determine the severity and pattern of abuse suffered by the victim. Bruises come in many different colors. A bruise that is red around the edges is a more superficial trauma than a darker purple-blue bruise that is a deeper injury and closest to the point of trauma impact. A medical examiner confirms this superficial analysis of the depth and color of the bruise by performing a cross-section incision.

And the color also has indications about when the trauma took place. If the bruise is yellow-brown in color, this means that the trauma happened at least eighteen hours earlier and is already in the healing process. Dr. Motte looks for all these kinds of bruises: "When I see a constellation of fresh, healing and healed injuries in my dead patients, and the occasional live patients I examine, I opine a series of abuse over a period of time rather than a onetime occurrence of abuse."[13] A pattern of abuse over time would also likely point homicide investigators toward individuals who were close to the victim. Unfortunately, the Guatemalan medical examiner failed to provide any analysis of these contusions or abrasions on Claudina Isabel's body. In general, the official autopsy provides no detailed explanation about her injuries, except to determine that Claudina Isabel died from a gunshot wound to the head.

(Mis)Handling of Evidence and Victims' Families

On September 6, 2005, at the request of the prosecutor, Mr. Velásquez provided hair samples from Claudina Isabel's hairbrush for comparison to hair samples taken from her clothing. The prosecutor's report erroneously concluded that the hair samples of "Jorge Velásquez" were the same as some of the samples taken from Claudina Isabel's clothing. Hair samples have never been taken from the main suspects—who seemed to change with each newly assigned investigator or prosecutor. The ballistic analysis fared no better. The ballistic report is dated February 2, 2005, and the MP stamped it "Received" with a date of February 28, 2005.[14] These dates are baffling given that when Mr. Velásquez confronted the chief prosecutor, Renato Durán, about these ballistics reports that were dated nearly six months prior to his daughter's murder, the prosecutor insisted that there were no mistakes. "You are mistaken. There is nothing wrong with the ballistics reports," he responded. When Mr. Velásquez showed the date stamps on the ballistics reports to the prosecutor, Durán shrugged his shoulders, tossed the papers back at Mr. Velásquez, and dismissed the significance, saying, "It is just a mistake. It does not mean anything. It is insignificant." When Mr. Velásquez suggested that these types of mistakes would make it easy for a defense lawyer to eliminate evidence, Durán again shrugged his shoulders. He also became increasingly agitated that I was silently taking notes throughout these meetings, as I had done since I first began to accompany Jorge.

In her comprehensive overview of the contours of feminicide in Guatemala when she was a Guatemalan congressional deputy (2004–8), Alba Estela Maldonado Guevara concluded that the victims and survivors of feminicide were subjected to revictimization by the Guatemalan authorities, who consistently treat those seeking justice with indifference, cruelty, and stigmatization and demonstrate a lack of political will to resolve the cases.[15] In meetings with the prosecutor, I was amazed at the blatant hostility displayed by him and his staff toward Jorge.

Instead of fomenting a culture of respect for victims and their families, the prosecutor overtly works to dismiss the victims' claims and dissuade the victims from pursuing justice. For example, in every single meeting I attended with Jorge, the prosecutor would become increasingly and visibly annoyed as Jorge inquired about follow-up investigative activities on his daughter's case since our previous meeting; there was generally a lapse of ten to fourteen days between these meetings. Invariably, the prosecutor would begin by stating, "If there are any problems prosecuting this case, it will be because you have taken the evidence to the public through the BBC and corrupted it." Then, inexplicably, he would blurt out, "The medical examiner's report indicates that your daughter was not a virgin and interviews with her friends indicate that she had been known to drink beer and may have even consumed cocaine." On the occasion of a joint meeting with Prosecutor Durán and his team charged with investigating

Claudina Isabel's murder, the chief investigator commented to Jorge as we were leaving the meeting, "I lost my aunt. They killed her. But the truth is that all these cases are very complicated, and I have to resign myself to the fact that it will never be resolved."[16]

Thus the prosecutor communicates to the victim's father that it is his fault as well as the BBC's that the murderer is not brought to justice, that it is his daughter's fault that she was killed, and that if Jorge was a more reasonable individual, he, like the prosecutor's chief investigator, would resign himself to the fact that his daughter's case, like 98 percent of feminicide cases in Guatemala, will not be resolved. Much to his credit, Jorge always maintained his calm and would reply to the prosecutor, "If the case is lost, it is because the Prosecutor's Office has not done its job. I am not saying my daughter was an angel. I am saying that young people should not have to pay with their lives for making a mistake or experimenting with life." Indeed, it is exactly these types of aspersions on the comportment of the deceased that stop many families from pushing for investigations of their murdered loved ones. Others fear reprisals from the perpetrators and rightly do not trust that the Prosecutor's Office can ensure their safety if they pursue justice.

When Durán was replaced as chief prosecutor by Alvaro Matus in March 2007, Matus denied Jorge's right to be accompanied by the professional of his choosing during meetings to discuss his daughter's case. Matus explicitly denied me entrance to their meeting. He greatly disliked the fact that I sat in these meetings in silence taking copious notes of everything that was said and only spoke to refer to notes from previous meetings if Jorge queried me about something someone had said. I still accompanied Jorge to meetings with Matus, who was visibly displeased that I continued to take notes while I waited in the reception area observing the comings and goings.

Matus dressed like a mobster in wide-shouldered, double-breasted suits and flashy ties. He gave a general impression of complete disregard for the suffering of Jorge and his family. On one occasion when Matus was late, Jorge called him on his cell phone. Matus was either dropping off or picking up his son or daughter at school. Jorge said, "What a luxury to be able to do that. Imagine what you would do if someone took that away from you." I remember thinking that Jorge was very brave.

In the Jane Doe case, the parents were forced to leave the country, though they continued to be harassed and threatened by those responsible for the death of their daughter and at the same time dismissed by those charged with investigating the case. When we were finally able to carry out a scientific autopsy under court order, MP staff charged with accompanying the family were, at best, dismissive. The MP psychologist whose job was to provide emotional support to the parents during the process of the autopsy dismissed their grief and suffering, at one point waving her hand at the girl's mother and saying, "Well, you haven't yet committed suicide."

The experiences of the families of Claudina Isabel Velásquez Paiz and Jane Doe are representative of those of the families of victims. Just as victims are blamed for their murders, their family members are blamed for the state's failure to advance the case, or the case is dismissed as not being a homicide even when all evidence points to it. For example, in the case of Jane Doe, the government of Guatemala continues to argue that she was not a homicide victim, even though forensic evidence unequivocally indicates homicide and the Inter-American Commission found her case to be such an aberrant abuse of power that it has been recommended to the Inter-American Court for judgment.

The experience of these families and countless others reaffirms UN Rapporteur Yakin Erturk's findings of a general climate in the criminal justice system as one lacking in respect for the dignity of survivors of violence and their families seeking justice. She specifically concluded that the system, instead of bringing justice to victims and their families, "merely revictimizes women." My experience working on these cases in Guatemala is that the justice system also victimizes families seeking justice. If they are not implicated in the execution of crimes, officials are implicated in the toleration of the crimes or the omission of their responsibilities to investigate and sanction criminal activities. Thus rather than support victims and their families, officials are ever ready to strike out at the families of victims or anyone who seeks to support their quest for justice, just like the criminals and clandestine groups implicated in the execution of the feminicides. Erturk stresses that the "blaming of the victims with little serious response to acts of violence against women exacerbates the suffering of the victims and that of their families; furthermore, it legitimizes the use of violence and awards the aggressor."[17]

In another report presented to the UN Commission on Human Rights in 2005, Erturk again noted that violence against women and the impunity enjoyed by its perpetrators was endemic to Guatemala and, further, that this fusion of violence against women and impunity reinforces structures of power, both state and non-state (often referred to as parallel powers in Guatemala). This, in turn, heightens citizen insecurity, foments fear, and decreases already waning confidence in state structures for the resolution of violence. This led her to conclude that the "major problem confronting the State is its inability to provide women with legal, judicial and institutional protection from violence."[18] Indeed, into the twenty-first century, the Guatemalan Penal Code exonerated rapists if they married their victims, provided the victims were over 12 years of age. This antiquated law sentencing rape victims to a life of punishment with their tormentors was finally overturned by the Guatemalan Constitutional Court in 2006.

2 *Esperanza's Story*
Sold at 12

Esperanza's father abandoned his family, leaving Esperanza,[1] her siblings, and her mother in abject poverty. In the absence of her father, Esperanza was first the property of her mother and brothers. Later she was the property of her husband, Francisco Juan, and his parents. Esperanza is illiterate, like 30 percent of women and girls in her Mam-Maya community in Huehuetenango.[2] Instead of going to school, Esperanza worked in the fields and performed household labor from her earliest memories. In her father's absence, her mother was the de facto head of household and had authority over decision making in her daughter's life. Esperanza had no recourse to protection when her mother sold her to 20-year-old Francisco Juan in 1994, two years before the 1996 Peace Accords were signed.

High in the Cuchumatán Mountains of Huehuetenango, Todos Santos appears bucolic to the many tourists who make the journey to witness the colorful, traditional clothing of men and women. Todos Santos is one of the few remaining Maya communities where the majority of Mam-Maya men still wear traditional clothes. Visitors photograph the smoke from wood-burning stoves rising above the red tile roofs of adobe houses, men in red-striped pants and hand-loomed shirts with intricate weavings, women in dark blue skirts with colorful woven *huipiles* (Maya blouses) carrying water on their heads in bright-colored plastic vessels. Tourists often miss the misery and memories of violence hidden behind all these colors.

When I first traveled to San Miguel Acatán (about forty miles from Todos Santos) in January 1990, we had to pass through numerous army-controlled Civil Defense Patrol (PAC) checkpoints at Chiantla, La Capellanía, and Paquix, among other places. Though some checkpoints were abandoned, the PACs were still present in these communities. To reach Todos Santos, one would have had to pass these same checkpoints until the fork in the road that leads to San Miguel Acatán.

Huehuetenango was a strategic area for the army because of its border with Mexico and the Pan-American Highway passing through it. So whoever controls this zone (then and now) controls movement of people, weapons, and commerce throughout the country and also has easy access to the capital. Militarily, this meant the PACs of San Miguel, Todos Santos, and other communities in this corridor were ferocious and powerful.

Scholars include the Huehuetenango region in discussions on rural lynchings in Guatemala—a phenomenon of apparently unorganized mob violence against defenseless targets. A Japanese tourist and tour bus driver were lynched in April 2000 amid rumors about satanic cult plans to carry out sacrificial rituals in the area. The lynching was a mob action, and no one was ever convicted of the killings.[3] The neoliberalizing Guatemalan state has played a central role in creating the conditions for the violence of lynchings. The state's response to the lynchings and other forms of mob violence that have risen as a "local practice" since the signing of the Peace Accords has been mostly silence. Marta Estela Gutiérrez and Paul Hans Kobrak conducted field research on lynchings in Huehuetenango. They were told that elders (called *principales* in traditional Mayan hierarchies) commonly ordered public floggings of men who refused paternal responsibility, women accused of sexual intercourse outside of marriage, and youths who insulted their elders.[4] So while some may romanticize *ley de costumbre* (Maya customary law) as somehow righting historic wrongs, the reality is that customary law most often deploys "tradition" to deny Indigenous women equal protection before the law while at the same time allowing the state to abdicate its responsibility to treat all citizens equally and further reinforces patriarchy at all institutional levels.

A comprehensive investigation conducted by the United Nations Mission in Guatemala (MINUGUA) concluded that the state's weak response had become a factor that both legitimized and justified lynchings: "The idea that lynchings are outside the reach of the law is viewed as a guarantee of impunity by those participating."[5] Indeed, one might argue that there is a two-tiered legal system in Guatemala: the state system serving elite interests through court action or lack thereof and customary law for poor Indigenous people that guarantees unequal access to the legal system—especially for women seeking protection from gender violence and access to property rights.

Before the genocide, this formidable patriarchal structure had some checks and balances within the local customs and religious practices in which everyone participated. The genocide, and the military occupation that followed, ruptured this system and further insulated families and family violence, especially violence against women, which was exacerbated by the violence of the PACs and the PTSD of victims and victimizers. Violence suffered within families became routine rather than an exceptional occurrence. And this violence followed patterns of power wherein the least powerful is the most abused.

The violence suffered under the genocide and at the height of PAC control set into action a spiral of violence as a source of conflict resolution that brought an escalation of gender violence within families, neighborhoods, and communities. This ambient violence emboldened men to see unaccompanied women and girls as their prey. And while girls are seen as burdens to the family, they are also commodities with an exchange value. Esperanza was sold to Francisco Juan without her consent. The payment was made from Francisco Juan to Esperanza's mother with no intention of Esperanza ever having access to the funds; this represents a payment for conjugal slavery. Francisco Juan bought himself a 12-year-old child to enslave as his "bride."

In the past, before the genocide, many Maya communities practiced arranged marriage. This is different from forced marriage. An arranged marriage is a union wherein children agree that their parents or a third party may arrange the marriage. In addition, an arranged marriage with the consent of both the bride and the groom requires that both parties have the right to a veto. A forced marriage is one in which either the bride or the groom or both are married without their consent or are coerced to consent, as was Esperanza's case.

Bridewealth is an amount of property or money given by the groom's family to the bride's family. It is understood as compensation to the bride's family for the loss of her labor and also as a kind of insurance for her future should the marriage end. Bridewealth does not necessarily mean that a marriage is arranged. That is to say, an arranged marriage can happen without bridewealth and bridewealth can be given in a marriage arranged by bride and groom.

While forced marriage may be presented by some as a form of arranged marriage, it is more akin to conjugal slavery, because the marriage is forced, without consent, and the bride has no veto power. Moreover, the same patriarchal structure that empowers a girl's parents to force her into marriage puts her under the absolute control of the man she is forced to marry. She is viewed as property passed from her parents to the man who will be her husband.

What at some point in the past may have been a practice of arranged marriage with or without bridewealth today in poor Maya communities is transactional conjugal slavery. Even girls and women who are not married in exchange for a fee are treated as a commodity belonging to the husband. They are also perceived as property, first by their parents and other immediate male relatives and then by whomever they are forced to marry or service. Girls can be forced or sold into marriage or service (in the fields or as an urban servant), just as young boys are contracted into plantation labor through an advance payment to the father. This leads the "buyer" to believe that the person is his property.

Francisco Juan was a 20-year-old man when he bought 12-year-old Esperanza and took her, screaming and crying, to his parents' home. While at first confused, she realized that she had been sold because her mother did not try to stop them from taking her and she had witnessed this happen to another girl in her community. When she reached Francisco Juan's home, his mother told Esperanza that she would be Francisco Juan's woman, his wife. She told her, "Don't worry. Stop crying. Everything will be fine."

For the first month, Francisco Juan seemed to be kind to Esperanza and would talk to her. But the conjugal slavery began when he raped her and verbally and physically abused her. "The first time he was on top of me, it hurt so much. I was just a girl," she remembers. "I didn't even know what sex was. I was bleeding, I never wanted to do it again." She was obligated to accept his sexual assaults as part of her "wifely" duties. There was no consent. She was not permitted to decline. She had no safe refuge, no place where she could simply be an autonomous human being outside the control of Francisco Juan or his family. She had nowhere to flee. She could not return home because her mother had sold her.

During the day, Esperanza was forced to perform household chores—cleaning and handwashing clothes. Francisco Juan's mother told Esperanza that she had to accept that this was the way her life would be. While Esperanza worked all day under his mother's watchful eye, Francisco Juan was away from the house. After their first month together, he began to arrive home drunk. Francisco Juan berated Esperanza and further abused her. He would enter their room in the middle of the night, drag her out of bed, and beat her. He subjected her to verbal, physical, and sexual abuse. His parents did nothing to intervene or stop the violence. In this way, Francisco Juan and his parents collectively subjected Esperanza to conjugal slavery and sexual violence.

Esperanza had no freedom of movement. She was not "allowed" to leave the house. She had no access to family resources and no say in how they were spent. Esperanza had no control over any aspect of her life and no one to protect her. She was abused by those who should have protected her. She knew she could not go to the police. She had no resources to pay any bribes, and the most likely outcome would have been that they would return her to Francisco Juan and his family or to her mother, who would have returned her to Francisco Juan because he had bought her. For three months, Esperanza was abused and assaulted near-daily by Francisco Juan. When asked why she did not go to the police, Esperanza explained, "The police are corrupt. They only help people who can pay a bribe. They would never help a Mam girl like me."

One night after a particularly bad beating, she made the decision to flee and ran away to her cousin Jacinto's home. He agreed to give her a safe place to stay for fear of her safety. He had plans to migrate to the United States. In 1994, at the age of 12, Esperanza had a choice of fending for herself in Guatemala or running away with her cousin to the safety of the United States. When they reached Florida, she once again began working in the fields. As in Guatemala, she did not have the opportunity to attend school, but she did have freedom of movement and was no longer subject to the violence of conjugal slavery.

At the age of 14, she met her current husband, Benjamin, with whom she now has five daughters. They married in Florida in 1998 when she was 16 years old; no parental consent was required. Her first child was born that same year. Child marriage remains legal in Florida and forty-three other US states. New York, New Jersey, Pennsylvania, Delaware, Minnesota, and Rhode Island are the only states with a minimum age of 18 with no exceptions. In twenty states, there is no minimum age for marriage with a parental or judicial waiver.[6] According to the National Coalition to End Child Marriage, nearly 300,000 children, some as young as 10, were married in the United States between 2000 and 2018.[7] Forced marriage and conjugal slavery are global human rights issues.

In 2015, two decades after her flight to the United States, Esperanza returned to Guatemala to help a very ill nephew. She stayed with him in the hospital for two weeks and accompanied him to his home when he was released. She walked to the pharmacy to buy his medicine and was shocked to hear a familiar voice move in close to her on the street and say, "You have to come back to be with me." She pulled away when Francisco Juan reached out to grab her arm. He became angry when she told him that she was married with children in the United States. He began to hit her, threatening that she would not escape again, that she had returned and again belonged to him. He violently hit her in the head and kicked her in the back when she fell to the ground. She was very afraid because he was carrying his machete. As strangers approached, he started to run away, but as he left he threatened Esperanza, telling her that she would never escape him and that he would kill her family.

The strangers took Esperanza to a church, where she spent the night, returning in the morning to her nephew's side to give him the medicine and bid him farewell. Twenty-one years after running away from Francisco Juan at the age of 12, Esperanza found herself running away from him again. As before, she was too fearful to go to the police, did not trust the police, and had no one else to turn to for protection or comfort. She took the threats seriously and again fled Guatemala. She returned to her family in the United States. More than two decades after she fled Francisco Juan's violence, Esperanza remains a victim to the hierarchy of abuse wherein he felt free to abuse and threaten her. This is because Francisco Juan still views Esperanza as his property, and he always will because he bought her.

Esperanza was right to take these threats seriously. Her community is a particularly dangerous place because previous army-controlled civil patrol structures have facilitated contemporary drug trafficking, organized crime, and gang activity. Compounding this with the regional history of lynchings makes it a very complicated place to live. Moreover, as is the case for many victims of violence, the Ministerio Público does not have an office in her community.

There are three offices of the MP for residents of Huehuetenango; they are located in the capital, Huehuetenango (1.5 hours by car), Santa Eulalia (2.5 hours by car), and La Democracia (3 hours by car). Irregular public transportation doubles the travel time. Poor rural women, often Indigenous, lack the resources and freedom of movement to travel to these offices that are far away both geographically and culturally. Moreover, none of these MP offices is a welcoming place for women who are victims of gender-based violence or threats. Esperanza would also be subject to intersectional discrimination: she is a rural peasant, a Maya woman, and a monolingual Mam speaker.

Pervasive public and private violence makes Guatemala a dangerous place for all women. Urban Huehuetenango is no safer for women, and they fare no better than their rural counterparts when seeking justice.[8] On July 30, 2015, 17-year-old Brenda Morales Leiva died in the Hospital Regional de Huhuetenango after unknown assailants forced her to consume a toxic substance. On February 22, 2016, Sherlyn Ramos, a 19-year-old student, received multiple bullet wounds on her way to school when her motorcycle was stolen from her just two blocks from a police station. The police were slow to respond to the shooting and claimed there was nothing they could do because they did not have an available police unit to assist the victim. It is unclear how long it took for the authorities to get her to the hospital. Despite surgical intervention, she died from the multiple gunshot wounds and trauma.[9] On March 3, 2016, students marched in Huehuetenango demanding an end to the violence against women and investigation into the killing of Sherlyn.[10] No suspects have been arrested for the murder of Sherlyn Ramos or Brenda Morales Leiva. In fact, it is not even certain that their murders are counted in the annual quantification of murdered women because they died in the hospital. The National Civilian Police (PNC) only count those found dead; it does not include in its homicide count those found injured who later die.

All these years after the murder of Claudina Isabel, urban, middle-class, female students are still unable to collectively claim justice for the killing of another urban woman student, and an illiterate Mam peasant woman has even less chance of getting justice. The murders of Claudina Isabel, Sherlyn, and Brenda, like the gender violence to which Esperanza was subjected and the threats she received, are examples of the endemic impunity and corruption in Guatemala that make justice intangible for women in general and young, poor, Indigenous women like Esperanza in particular. Moreover, the conflation of Esperanza's age, gender, socioeconomic status, Indigenous identity, Spanish-language incapacity, and discrimination against Mam-language speakers makes her possibility of accessing justice nil. Impunity, corruption, and discrimination nurture public and private violence against women and are major drivers of immigration to the United States.

Victim Precipitation

Nor does educated, middle-class, ladina standing guarantee any semblance of justice.[11] Even those specifically charged with investigating and bringing to justice perpetrators of violence against women are woefully unsuccessful. In 2005, the year Claudina Isabel was murdered, the Women's Section of the Prosecutor's Office and the special police unit assigned to violence against women both openly admitted to the UN Rapporteur that "40 percent of the cases are filed and never investigated."[12] A 2016 study by the United Nations Commission against Impunity in Guatemala (CICIG) showed that in 2015–16, only 43 percent of gender violence cases were even accepted by the Prosecutor's Office, meaning that 57 percent of the cases were never investigated at all.[13] And those cases that are investigated tend to focus suspicion on the murdered women, following an old, largely discredited school of criminal investigation known as "victim precipitation,"[14] which seeks to identify what the victim did to cause her victimization rather than develop the profile of the perpetrator. It also makes it easy for investigators to draw conclusions about homicide cases without a proper investigation.

Prosecutors and police presume that certain *kinds* of women, such as prostitutes, do not deserve protection and have no rights. So when they encounter a crime against a woman, that attitude combines with a "blame the victim" mentality, allowing them to dismiss the victim as someone whose death does not merit investigation. The slightest details, like Claudina Isabel's sandals and navel ring, lead them to conclude that the victim was a prostitute. And even if they are proved wrong, they still insist that sexual freedom must be the cause of death, claiming that the victim went to meet a boyfriend or had sneaked out to meet a man. They treat women as responsible for their own murders.

Sometime in 2006, a 14-year-old girl tells her mother that she is going to the corner store to buy aspirin. She never returns. Her body is later found lifeless, with marks of torture. This is a real murder case of a Guatemala City girl who disappeared from her neighborhood in the afternoon. The prosecution's investigator assigned to this case told me that despite the fact that he had no evidence to support his theory, he was certain that the girl had "lied to her mother" and "gone to meet her boyfriend."[15] When I asked the investigator if he had interviewed any of her friends or neighbors to determine who this boyfriend might be, he responded that he planned to interview her family but had not yet done any interviews—and this was nearly one year after her murder. This did not stop him from further justifying his theory of the lying daughter sneaking off to meet her boyfriend: "After so many years in this business, an experienced investigator like me just knows."

Whatever this investigator's intuition may or may not have told him, the MP has a miserable record of conviction.[16] After more than 400 murders of Guatemalan women in the first eleven months of 2004, only 15 warrants to arrest 15 suspects had been issued by the MP. In February 2005, there were some 72 murder suspects detained, but none had gone to trial.[17] Claudina Isabel and Jane Doe were among the 5,338 women and men registered as homicides in 2005; that same year, the MP obtained a grand total of eight murder convictions.[18] As an exasperated UN Rapporteur Philip Alston concluded in his February 2007 report on Guatemala, "With a criminal justice system unable to achieve more than a single-digit conviction rate for murder, the State bears responsibility under human rights law for the many who have been murdered by private individuals."[19]

Articles that fill the daily papers with news of murdered girls and women tend to be short, with the final line stating that the victim had a belly button ring or tattoos—both of which signal to the reader that the victim was a gang member or prostitute. An article about Claudina Isabel was published in the Guatemala City newspaper *La Hora* on August 13, 2005. It stated:

> A woman was attacked by gunfire from unknown people who intercepted her on 10th Avenue and 9th Street of Colonia Roosevelt, Zone 11. Neighbors notified the voluntary firefighters, who attempted to resuscitate her, but she died. The Prosecutor's Office was unable to identify her because she did not carry any documents. She was wearing black sandals, blue pants, a black shirt and pink sweater. The medical examiner indicated she was 18 years old and that her death was instantaneous due to two bullet wounds to the head. Agents of the National Civilian Police carried out a search for those who committed the crime but had negative results.[20]

So who killed Claudina Isabel? Most likely someone she knew. There are several suspects, but discussing them and the evidence against them could jeopardize whatever possible case might be carried forward in Guatemalan courts. Still, we can think about Claudina Isabel's case within the larger phenomenon of the killing of women in Guatemala.

Why Feminicide?

If Claudina Isabel was killed by someone who knew her, why place her murder in the category of feminicide? What is feminicide, and does the term help explain the phenomenon or further obfuscate it? In criminology literature, the term "femicide" refers to the murder of women.[21] In feminist literature, femicide refers to the killing of women by men because they are women.[22] Feminicide encompasses more than femicide because it holds responsible not only the male perpetrators but also the state and judicial structures that normalize misogyny. Feminicide is a political term. Impunity, silence, and indifference each play a role in feminicide. Thinking about feminicide helps unpack belief systems that place violence based on gender inequality within the private sphere;[23] it also reveals the very social character of the killing of women as a product of relations of power between men and women. Thinking about the killing of women as feminicide also allows us to question the usefulness of legal, political, and cultural analyses of governmental and societal responses to the killing of women. Thinking about feminicide leads us back to the foundations of power and implicates the state as a responsible party. That is to say, the government has responsibility for the killing of women whether by commission of the actual crime, toleration of the violence, or omission of its responsibility to investigate and prosecute homicides.[24] In Guatemala, feminicide is a crime that exists because of the absence of guarantees to protect the rights of women and the lack of political will to recognize women as full citizens.

A 2001 study on femicide in Canada revealed that women are more likely to be murdered by men. Over a twenty-year period in Ontario, men were the perpetrators of 98 percent of the 1,206 murders of women. As elsewhere in the world, men are also more likely to be killed by men. Indeed, despite the media preoccupation with women killing their husbands, more than 50 percent of the murdered women were victims of spousal homicide, whereas less than 10 percent of male victims were killed by a spouse. The Ontario study concluded that the killing of men is driven by the way men relate to men but that the killing of women is a "problem of relations between men and women."[25] Still, while these murders may be categorized as femicide because 98 percent of the women were killed by men and these murders were gendered, they do not constitute feminicide because, while the state may not have adequately protected the women and prevented the murders from taking place, the Ontario authorities did resolve 93 percent of the murders.[26]

Feminicide: Violence against Women and Girls in Guatemala

Violence against women serves to reinforce patriarchal norms and male dominance by rendering women unsafe and insisting that women's own actions are to blame for the violence perpetrated against them. In Guatemala, feminicide has been taking place for years, on a massive scale. This has happened because of an absence of guarantees of the rights and safety of women and because of a social and political culture that places the blame for crimes against women on the women themselves rather than on the perpetrators.

In a way, this is consistent with most Guatemalans' attitudes toward crime. Whenever they hear that someone has been the victim of a crime, their first impulse is always to say that the person/victim "andaba en algo"—was involved in something. This colloquialism dates back to La Violencia (The Violence, referring to the genocidal period of state terror), because that belief allowed people to protect themselves psychologically from the violence that surrounded them.

Jorge and I used to talk about violence in Guatemalan society and the ways in which people become accustomed to witnessing violence and living in terror. One day we were talking about the ease with which victims are blamed for their own killing as a way to separate them from the rest of society. I suggested this was a continuation of La Violencia. For instance, if a person saw security troops dragging his neighbor's teenage daughter from her home and later her body was found with signs of torture, then it was easier for the neighbor to believe that it happened because she was involved in something she shouldn't have been. Because if she wasn't, then that would mean that *his* teenage daughters could also be at risk, and he wanted to believe that if they don't do anything they're not supposed to do, then everything will be okay. The alternative—the possibility of his daughters being dragged off to be tortured and murdered—would be too horrible to contemplate.

I asked Jorge if he had ever witnessed army violence during the genocidal dictatorships. Always thoughtful, he considered my query, then responded, "I had almost forgotten. But, yes, I did see someone taken away. I was living near the medical school in the early 1980s. I got home late at night and saw someone being dragged away. I quickly went inside my apartment. At the time, I assumed he must have been a subversive and forgot about it."

This attitude persists today. For instance, I remember one case where two brothers were murdered—machine-gunned to death—during the day at the entrance to one of the best private schools in Guatemala City. And as soon as that happened, everyone asked, "I wonder what the father does?" Immediately they presumed that the victims' family must be responsible. They didn't ask about the predators who kill children. They asked what the victims or their parents did to cause it: How did they break the rules?

This attitude is even more powerful when it comes to crimes against women, because it combines with traditional societal attitudes about women. So if a man gets murdered, people may assume that he has done something to offend a gang or other violent group, but it would have to be *something*: maybe he refused a direct order or hurt one of their family members or took money from them. For women, it is different. People are willing to believe that just living a free life, having a boyfriend, or wearing sandals is enough to "cause" a murder, and even to excuse it.

A Vanderbilt study identifies Guatemala as the country in Latin America with the highest tolerance of violence against women suspected of infidelity, with 58 percent of those surveyed saying they regarded infidelity as a justification for violence.[27] These contemporary legacies of state violence from the genocide to the present are also evident in family relations and specifically in practices of violence against women. Guatemalan women find themselves trapped in oppressive and violent relationships because of the widespread social acceptance of violence against women. Men hold the monopoly on the use of this violence, and women and girls are their property and victims.

The misogynistic attitudes work in the opposite direction too for men who want to protect the women they love. The blame-the-victim perspective makes it legitimate for men to limit the freedom of their wives, daughters, and sisters in order to protect them. If responsibility for preventing violence lies with the potential victim rather than the potential perpetrator, then it becomes legitimate to limit women's freedom more and more.

I have spoken to many men who tell me proudly that the women in *their* family will not be at risk of feminicide because they do not let them leave the house without permission and male accompaniment. I do not doubt that they are doing this out of love and a desire to protect them, but these are adult women, not children, and their lives are curtailed completely as their social space collapses. Yet the men in their lives believe that if they "let" their sister or daughter go out alone to work or socialize, and something happens to her, then it would be their fault too, because they would have allowed it to happen. If he had just kept her at home, inside, she would have been safe. This, of course, is predicated on the fear of an unknown assailant when in reality women all over the world are most likely to be killed by men they know.

In Guatemala, the killings of women increase with impunity that at its minimum is an absence of punishment for perpetrators; this generates a highly insecure environment. As Ana María Méndez told me, "Impunity has the face of a woman," meaning impunity is embodied and experienced in the insecurity and fear women carry. She explains:

I did not really understand what it meant to be a woman in Guatemala until Claudina Isabel was murdered. I understood what it meant when I read that my friend's murder—we did not yet have the legal term femicide—wasn't worthy of investigation. I understood when I read the medical examiner's report that stated that my friend could not be sexually assaulted because she had previously had sexual relations. I understood what it meant to be a woman in Guatemala when no government authority had any interest in finding out who had kidnapped, beaten, and raped her. I understood when her case remained in impunity, like so many other Claudinas.[28]

It is this insecurity and lack of official recognition of gender violence that makes Guatemalan women fearful of taking a bus or meeting a friend for coffee. When asked if he worried about his adult sister's safety in Guatemala City, one friend responded, "Not even to the corner store without permission. We are not going to let anything happen to her." While the brother was proud of the way he was "protecting" his sister from any possible assailants, this attitude is itself a product of patriarchy and misogyny. His sister, a 23-year-old college student, was experiencing the fallout of the Guatemalan feminicide—a collapsing of social space and loss of freedom of movement. As Yakin Erturk notes, it is paradoxical that men's honor "is intrinsically associated with their ability to guard the sexuality of women with whom they are associated," yet, at the same time, the "violation of the sexuality of other women such as in rape is also a manifestation of the way in which masculine power establishes domination over women."[29] In their daily lives, Guatemalan women are constricted and defined by this domination in the private and public spheres.

3   Cycles of Violence

Between 1980 and 1983, the Guatemalan army carried out a planned genocide of Indigenous Maya communities. During the span of the thirty-six years of war (1960-96), the country witnessed unspeakable atrocities perpetrated primarily by government and military forces against rural Maya communities in the highland regions of the country and against any identified or suspected dissidents in urban areas. The Guatemalan truth commission attributed responsibility for 93 percent of the atrocities to the Guatemalan army.[1]

The military government's conceptualization of antigovernment guerrillas became synonymous with Indigenous Guatemalans. The government developed a preemptive strategy and engaged in a "scorched earth" campaign during which they systematically burned, tortured, raped, and terrorized into submission Guatemala's Indigenous population. This preemptive genocide was carried out to prevent the possibility of dissent and revolution.

Whole villages were massacred. Men were rounded up, shot, and buried in mass graves. Men, women, and children were also rounded up and forced into churches, which were then burned to the ground.[2] Once the massacres took place, all the remaining structures in that community would be burned to the ground, and the military would destroy all the food crops so that any massacre survivors would be left without homes or food. As one massacre survivor told me, "They even killed the dogs. If it moved, they killed it." By the end of the scorched earth campaign, over 626 Maya villages had been burned to the ground, their residents massacred. Maya women survivors were rounded up and frequently held captive as sexual slaves at army bases or villages. Maya women would be required to "deliver tortillas" to the local army base, which was a euphemism for presenting themselves for what the army referred to as "recreation" for the soldiers: rape of Indigenous women. When I have asked women why they would present themselves knowing they would be gang-raped, the response was always that they knew if they did not go, the army would come to take their young daughters.[3] Indeed, thousands of women were subjected to sexual violence and torture prior to being assassinated by state agents. In fact, the report of the Commission for Historical Clarification confirms that the state trained its soldiers and other armed agents to rape and to terrorize women. During the war, army soldiers and other security officers were responsible for 94.3 percent of all sexual violence against women.[4] What does it mean to grow up in this ambient terror and its aftermath?

Children of Genocide

The children who experienced and survived the violence during the genocide, as well as those who were born as it came to an end, were subject to unique suffering. First, the children experienced the violence in a personal, deeply held way. Too young to understand the sociopolitical aspects of the violence into which they were born or to be able to connect the violence to larger themes, the children experienced the violence as personal. As the army continued to control villages up to the signing of the Peace Accords in December 1996, children born in the 1980s and 1990s witnessed firsthand the government invading their homes; torturing their parents, relatives, and neighbors; killing them; raping their mothers and sisters; and burning their homes, livestock, and means of survival. They experienced their government intending their death and destroying their culture. And they lived under constant army surveillance. One survivor who was 10 when his village was massacred told me the soldiers would shout, "Es la ley" (It is the law), as they ran through his village shooting men, women, and children and burning their homes. Until he became bilingual in Spanish, he thought "Es la ley" meant the soldiers had the right to destroy his village and kill his family.

On my first trip to the Cuchumatán Mountains in January 1990, we passed through numerous abandoned PAC checkpoints. As we ventured into communities in the interior of the department, we were told by locals that the PACs were not demobilized even in places where the checkpoints were abandoned. Declassified US documents corroborate the local experience of militarization. For example, a declassified 1991 US Defense Intelligence Agency (DIA) cable assessing Guatemalan troops reports that Colonel Víctor Manuel Ventura gave a secret security briefing on the structure of the Guatemalan army that included 40,000 active army personnel, one 250-person company of army reserves for each of the twenty-two departments, and 3,934 active PAC groups with 546,000 members—15,000 of whom were armed.[5]

In our 1990 trip, we witnessed a humble home recently burned out, with a Guatemalan flag flying above. My friend Phyllis and I were on our way to visit relatives of our friend Ana, a Kanjobal Maya refugee then living in California. It was a thirteen-hour bus trip from Huehuetenango. We were the only non-Kanjobal on the bus. Only when we arrived in San Miguel Acatán did we discover that this was the community where Sister Dianna Ortiz, a US nun, had taught children in a local school. In November 1989, Sister Dianna was kidnapped by security forces in Guatemala City and brutally tortured.[6]

After her escape, she returned to the United States. In San Miguel Acatán, the school sat silent. In a nearby patio, a statue of the Virgin Mary had been wrapped in a vine of thorns. "This is to protect the virgin until the violence passes," explained one of our friends.

Magda's Story

San Miguel Acatán and other highland villages suffered sustained and systematic regimes of terror under the army's security structures. Magda's nearby village in Huehuetenango did not escape this violence.[7] In fact, her village, like San Miguel Acatán, was among the first wave of communities in the area forced to submit to participation in the army-controlled civil patrols and live under the dominion of the army. This resulted in tremendous violence against community members, including army roundups of local civilians who were then presented to the local civil patrol, which under army orders was forced to kill and bury the men in mass graves.[8] These civil patrol structures left indelible marks on community organization. The combination of war and gender-based discrimination are among the factors that nurture a culture of violence in which men, whether security forces or judicial officers, believe that women are their property to do with what they wish. Guatemala is a society where virility and strength (including the protection and discipline of women and children) continue to be markers of macho male identity.

The Civil Patrol was not demobilized until 1997, as part of the 1996 Peace Accords. Many years later, children born after the genocidal massacres lived with the constant fear of the PAC or of demobilized PAC reprisal, as well as the dread and pain carried by their parents who in Western terms suffer from severe PTSD. The children of survivors experienced a profound dislocation wherein their rhythms of life were entirely disoriented. The displacement of over 1.5 million men, women, and children (nearly one of every eight

Guatemalans) in Guatemala due to the three-decade war and genocide disproportionately affected Indigenous women and children, particularly young children. As massacre survivors fled from their destroyed villages into the remote highlands, or toward Mexico, mothers were often encouraged to abandon their children, who were seen as a threat to the safety of the fleeing group as they moved at a slower pace and had less ability to withstand hunger and thirst. Moreover, children were targeted by the army as a way to locate villages in flight. Former soldiers told me they would listen for crying children, then fire their machine guns and shoot mortars in that direction. The army's term for this was "hunting the deer."

Children were also targeted for forced recruitment into the Guatemalan army as well as the civil patrols, where they received arms training and were forced to follow Guatemalan army orders. Orphans were numerous because the military killed parents in village massacres or attacks on communities in flight.[9] Many families were separated as they fled army attacks, and many people died from starvation and exposure to the elements while struggling to survive running from one wooded area to another for years. Older siblings became guardians without knowledge or capacity. Educational systems were destroyed. The ability to pass down vital family and cultural knowledge from one generation to the next was irrevocably interrupted. It was a highly successful genocide that sought to destroy Maya communities, force displacement on those who survived, and impair the capacity of internally displaced Maya and refugees to maintain their culture and rebuild their communities.

The impact of displacement was profound. The children experienced dire conditions fleeing the army in the mountains and struggling to survive in refugee camps in Mexico. Daily survival was marked by overcrowding, food shortages, lack of shelter, poor sanitation, a disintegrated family support structure, a ruptured social network, and isolation. For these children, the impacts of the genocide were compounded one on the other. Daily life was punctuated by hunger, exposure to the elements, inadequate shelter, lack of clothing, illness without medicine, no formal education, and certainly a deep sorrow from the daily accretion of fear, rejection, and exclusion. These experiences left an indelible mark on the generation of Guatemalan children who grew up during the genocide and in its immediate aftermath.

The conflation of poverty, post-genocide violence, and a broken generation of genocide survivors exacerbated familial, intimate partner, and community violence. The army's recourse to violence is repeated in different ways throughout Guatemalan society. Those with the least power, women and girls, have the least recourse to the use of violence for conflict resolution. Women and girls are most often on the receiving end of this violence because they have the least power in both the public and private spheres.

Moreover, within many Maya families, after the father, the eldest son is the effective head of household, and everyone in the household answers to him. This is to prepare him to be the head of family in the future. Within families, 90 percent of victims of intrafamilial violence are women and girls and 88 percent report that this violence includes physical violence.[10] Thus intrafamilial violence is violence against women.

For girls who are orphaned or abandoned, abuse is often the norm. Such was the experience of Magda, whose father abandoned her family when she was 10 years old and her sister was 12. After her paternal uncle took in the girls and their mother, he immediately became abusive. The girls were forced to leave school and begin working. The uncle sexually assaulted them and threatened to traffic them if they told anyone. Magda escaped by marriage to a man who became abusive. She fled this marriage and entered into a common-law marriage with another man with whom she had two children. While he initially seemed kind, he too became an abuser. In each situation, Magda was viewed as property by the men who dominated her: her father, her uncle, her husband, and the father of her children. She had the lowest position in the pecking order in each household and was at risk for abuse from any male in the household as well as any older female siblings of the men. Magda lived in a village in Huehuetenango, but her lived experience is similar to that of other women and girls throughout rural Guatemala.

Poor rural women and girls are expected to walk to the river or public well or other water source and bring water back to the house for drinking, cooking, cleaning, and bathing. They must feed the chickens, clean the chicken coop, and collect the eggs (if they are lucky enough to have any chickens). They are responsible for the care and feeding of any domestic animals or livestock (if they are fortunate enough to have any). This means milking the cows or goats and making cheese. They also cure and dry meat. They are responsible for the care, cleaning, and feeding of their children and their younger siblings. They must handwash the family's clothes at the river, which can be fifteen minutes to an hour away (and they have to carry the clothes there and back). If they are lucky, they have a water pipe or access to the community *pila* (communal washing area). They sweep dirt floors. They sweep dirt patios. They sew their own clothes and mend the men's clothing.

Guatemalan girls and boys work from a very young age. Indeed, 67 percent of children between 7 and 14 work in agricultural production—planting and harvesting corn, beans, sugarcane, coffee, and broccoli. Corn and beans are for household consumption. Coffee and sugarcane are grown for export in industrial plantations where children have been sold into labor by their families, work alone in exchange for minimal food, or work alongside their families. All child laborers work in abysmal conditions and under threat of corporal punishment at the whim of their parent or the plantation foreman. Another 24 percent of children between 7 and 14 years of age work in the service sector—cleaning houses, handwashing clothes, sweeping streets, collecting garbage, street vending, begging, and shining shoes. The US Department of Labor places forced agricultural labor and domestic labor at the top of its Categorical Worst Forms of Child Labor list. Further, it points to the prevalence of commercial exploitation of children and trafficking of children in Guatemala.[11]

Further corroborating these findings, the International Labor Organization (ILO) report on human trafficking and forced labor found that most forced labor in Guatemala is in agriculture and domestic service and that forced labor was most common in the Altiplano region (where Magda's village is located). The report found that Indigenous people are most vulnerable to forced labor because 73 percent are poor and 26 percent are extremely poor. It cited an ILO survey of four departments that found one in four households was affected by the forced labor of one or more of its members. Further, it concluded that the extreme poverty of Indigenous people renders them extremely dependent on their employers and "vulnerable to abusive working conditions."[12]

This dynamic of vulnerability and abuse is repeated within the hierarchy of the family. It is gendered: women have less power than men, girls less than boys. And it is patriarchal: the male head of household makes all decisions, and his offspring must abide by and enforce his decisions. This means that girls and women who marry into the family have less value and lower status than the already low status of the girl children of the patriarch. It also means that girls and/or women who are sold, married, or become domestic partners of family members must obey the orders of the patriarch as well as his offspring. Any deviation from the rules is subject to punishment.

Thus, in the absence of her father, Magda's uncle was the head of household in her childhood and able to repeatedly subject Magda and her sister to sexual violence. Neither the girls nor their mother had any recourse to protection. The 2014 ILO report notes that her Huehuetenango community has among the lowest human development indicators in the country and that 4 of 10 women and girls have been subjected to gender violence. Further, the ILO notes 2,626 reported cases of sexual violence, with only 9 cases that were investigated and sentenced in the department of Huehuetenango.[13] Magda's uncle viewed Magda and her sisters as his property by virtue of his role as the patriarch in the family and utilized his power to take exactly what he wanted from them.

After Magda's father abandoned the family and stopped providing financial support, Magda quit school to work. Magda, like other rural women and girls, was the first to rise to start a fire and begin making tortillas by rolling out the corn and hand-patting each of the tortillas by candlelight when they could afford to buy candles. Poor rural women prepare meals for families of twelve with food for two. When the meal is ready, the patriarch eats first, his sons eat second, his daughters eat third, his favored grandsons eat fourth, the patriarch's wife and her favorites eat next, and the wives of his sons and their children get whatever is left over in the same descending order. I have witnessed the youngest adopted daughter, who did not even have a seat at the family table, be given the leftover chicken wing bone to chew on while standing at mealtime. All resources are distributed in this hierarchical manner, and women have no control of income or family wealth.

Magda is ladina, which means that she is descended from Maya and non-Maya, but she has no Maya identity. Guatemala is a country divided by three basic groups: Maya, ladino, and criollo (descendants of Spaniards). On the Caribbean coast, there are also the Garifuna Afro-Guatemalans. The criollos continue to dominate the country and own most of it. Many criollos trace their ancestors to the original Spaniards. For example, former president Álvaro Arzú traced his lineage back to Pedro de Alvarado, conquistador of the Kingdom of

Guatemala in 1524.[14] Within the contemporary racial hierarchy, rural ladinas are discriminated against much in the same way as rural Maya women, unless they are educated and come from a family with land and resources.

Magda's Experience

Magda's experiences resonate with the hundreds of testimonies I have taken from women in Guatemala. Many rural widows have told me they chose to live in extreme poverty rather than to bring a stepfather into the home because stepfathers sexually abuse stepdaughters. I have witnessed that violence comes in many forms. Once while I interviewed the patriarch of a family, he berated his wife for not having his meal ready just two hours after she had had a tooth extracted with no anesthesia.

As a child, Magda lived in levels of violence, abuse, and degradation that are difficult to comprehend. Magda's uncle viewed her as his property. Magda had no social welfare system to call upon for help. Living in a state of impunity, her uncle raped her and threatened to kill her or sell her if she did not do what he demanded. Given the high rate of sexual trafficking of children in Guatemala, Magda had reason to fear that her uncle would make good on his threats. So she remained in this abusive environment until she married. Shortly after her wedding, her husband, Lucas, abused her because he considered her "used goods." Rather than offer compassion because of the abuse she had suffered under the dominion of her uncle, her husband berated her and used that very abuse as his excuse for mistreating her. He would push and hit her in private and public, telling her she was "useless" and "worth nothing." Magda believed him because she felt ashamed of the past abuse at the hands of her uncle.

During their three-year marriage, Magda's husband subjected her to conjugal slavery. Many women have described their marriage as a condition of ongoing rape. Many women have told me they were raped on their wedding night. The men tell them that they must fulfill their obligation (which is to submit to unwanted sexual assaults by their husbands). Still, even though he was abusive, Magda was frightened to be alone when her husband left her, because she feared more unknown violence might befall her.

Magda is a ladina who entered into a domestic partnership with Lucas, a K'iche' Maya; this is unusual but not unheard of. For many K'iche' men, it is an expression of power because of the racial hierarchy that places all ladinos above all Maya. Magda initially perceived Lucas as very protective and an escape from her uncle's abuse, even if Lucas held that against her. But Lucas has a drinking problem and lost his job shortly after Magda moved into his home with his family.

Lucas, his mother, and his sisters abused Magda. The mother and sisters disliked Magda because she was not K'iche' and they were ashamed of Lucas for bringing her home and having children with her. Magda was subjected to the hierarchy of abuse in the patriarchal home. Her husband continued to rule the household and became even more abusive after he lost his job. The abuse reached a critical point, and, fearing for her life, Magda sought assistance from the police.

Magda's Police Report and Restraining Order

On May 22, 2010, Magda made a complaint about physical abuse at the local police station in the town where she had moved with Lucas. The police complaint states that Magda denounced that while she was nursing their 8-month-old baby, Lucas arrived and "without provocation" began screaming and yelling "sinful" words at her and threw her out of the house. It also states that she has been subjected to physical aggression and threats by Lucas and his family, including the threat to take away her baby son. This complaint is signed by the police officer who composed it.

The same day, the justice of the peace issued a restraining order based on finding Lucas guilty of "intrafamily violence." The order prohibits Lucas from "perturbing or intimidating" Magda and also prohibits Lucas from "access to the home of Señora Magda . . . or her place of work or study." This restraining order was immediately effective for six months. According to the law, if Lucas were to violate the order, he would be guilty of "disobedience."

While the justice of the peace may have had good intentions ordering protective measures, he made a serious mistake because violence against women in Guatemala is no longer categorized as intrafamily violence. Under the 2008 Femicide Law, intrafamily violence is now categorized as violence against women and femicide in recognition of unequal power relations and ongoing gender inequality. Magda's situation should have been classified as violence against women under the Femicide Law. The term "intrafamily violence" can only be used to obtain the restraining order; it is not a legal category for a crime, whereas violence against women is. Therefore, though perhaps well meaning, the justice of the peace misapplied the Femicide Law.

In general, Guatemala continues to function like a colonial state. Everything is done on paper in what I call "bureaucratic proceduralism"—which means that while all documents are duly completed, paying attention to filling in the blanks and citing laws and procedures, whatever is contained in the document stays there. So a restraining order is simply one more document to complete and file. It is not an order to be carried out. No one will be instructed to protect Magda, who will simply be given a copy of the restraining order.

And in Magda's particular situation, the restraining order has serious consequences for her because Lucas is a former police officer and has cousins who are police officers. This means that Lucas most likely knew she had gone to the police before she even met with the justice of the peace. In the fraternity of the profession, it also means that those police officers were going to protect Lucas before they protect her.

And his town is a dangerous place. It is part of Pacific Route CA-02 (also referred to as the Corridor of Violence) that passes through Escuintla, Suchitepéquez, Retalhuleu, Quetzaltenango, and San Marcos up to the Mexican border. As a result, it is one of the fifteen most violent municipalities in the country.[15] It has the third highest rate of domestic violence (violence against women) in Guatemala and the fourth highest rate of violence against children.[16]

Until passage of the 2008 Femicide Law, it was legal for men to rape their wives, and until 2006, if a man raped a woman or a girl over 12 he could avoid punishment if he married her. So a girl or young woman could be forced to marry her rapist so that he wouldn't go to jail and she wouldn't "dishonor" her family. Not that many people actually go to jail or that men go to jail for rape, because they don't. There have been some important reforms in the judicial system since the passage of the Femicide Law: a new femicide unit in the police department in Guatemala City, a new special victims unit for the court, some specifically appointed femicide investigators (in Guatemala City), and the law cited by the justice of the peace in her ruling on Magda's case. But the problem for Magda (and other Guatemalan women and girl victims of gender violence, domestic violence, and intragenerational violence) is that beyond the judge citing the law, it only kicks in to concretely support women after they are dead.

Guatemalan law in general—and the Femicide Law in particular—are not constructed to prevent violence against women or intervene on behalf of women who have been raped and subjected to other forms of gender violence. Even after they are dead, there is only a 2 percent prosecution rate. So all these reforms help only 2 percent of women and then only after they are dead.[17]

There is no witness protection program; there is an inadequate structure for people who work in the court system and for police who actually want to do their jobs. For Magda, this means that she left the court with a piece of paper and nowhere to go with her baby and young daughter. There is no women's shelter where she could seek safe haven. Lucas's mother and sisters were certainly not going to support her efforts. So the restraining order exists on paper and is only meaningful when the Guatemalan government prepares its statistics on its protection of the rights of women and adds her restraining order to the many others that have been handed out. But in real life, in Magda's life, it is meaningless.

Lucas's Incident Report

A private lawyer hired by Lucas filed an incident report with a different justice of the peace. This report is not a court order; it is a challenge to the protective measures in the restraining order Magda received. By accepting the incident report filed by Lucas's lawyer, the justice of the peace nullified the previous protective measures of the restraining order. While Magda did not have a lawyer at any point because she lacks resources and has no institution to turn to for support, Lucas turned to the institution of the National Civilian Police and their lawyers.

Here again, the Femicide Law is not being applied. The justice of the peace has officially received an incident report that directly violates the Femicide Law. Both Lucas's lawyer and the justice of the peace, by receiving the incident report, have violated the Femicide Law simply by blaming the victim. The justice of the peace has discretion to receive or refuse this type of document. As this is a different justice of the peace from the one who established the protective measures, I imagine Lucas's lawyer has a professional relationship with this justice of the peace. This type of discretion combined with the lack of checks and balances in the Guatemalan legal system reveal why bureaucratic proceduralism is so dangerous to the rule of law.

Through this incident report, Lucas blames Magda and her "bad character" for "family violence," with no evidence presented to demonstrate that there was any violence on her part. There is no scientific evidence, no photographs, no psychological profile that a private lawyer would present when representing a client. Lucas and his lawyer use victim precipitation (blaming the victim) as evidence and cause for the violence Lucas committed. Interestingly, the document never denies that Lucas committed violence.

Under the Femicide Law, the state (and its representatives) is technically responsible for preventing violence against women. Further, it has the obligation to modify or stop any unjustified application of negative gender stereotypes. A restraining order is temporary and intended to decrease the risk factors of violence against women in order to protect the human rights of victims. To remove the restraining order in the face of repeated complaints against Lucas directly violates the spirit of the Femicide Law. Furthermore, the complaint lists the claims made by Lucas and his mother against Magda for having "bad character," being "jealous" and "aggressive," and "constantly having problems with family members." Blaming Magda in this way for Lucas's violence is the application of negative stereotypes to justify violence against women. Under the Femicide Law, this is not only insufficient reason to annul the restraining order; the claims are in and of themselves a violation of the Femicide Law.[18]

In Magda's life, this is a frightening document because by virtue of being represented by a lawyer, Lucas has been able to have the restraining order annulled. This serves to further intimidate Magda because it also makes clear that the legal system is not going to protect her and that the very laws established to protect women from violence can be misapplied and used against her. Magda has no-where to go for protection. While the Guatemalan government has annulled the antiquated rape law and passed the Femicide Law to protect the rights of women in Guatemala, it is largely unable to protect women from being victimized and has an abysmal record of prosecuting men for beating, raping, torturing, and killing women.

Feeling both abandoned by the Guatemalan government and trapped by Lucas, Magda fled to the United States seeking safe haven for herself and her baby. Magda received political asylum in the United States shortly before the election of Donald Trump. Had she arrived at the border during the Trump administration, US Border Patrol officers would have forcibly removed her nursing baby from her arms, separating mother and child. The baby would have been warehoused in abysmal conditions with other frightened children also separated from their parents. In June 2019, Bill Ong Hing, University of San Francisco law professor and founder of the Immigrant Legal Resource Center, described his conversations with teen mothers with infants and children ranging in age from 4 to 15 at a Border Patrol processing facility in Clint, Texas.

> Several cried as they talked about conditions and missing their parents. They cried, I teared up. However, I cried hard two times[,] . . . once when a six year old girl who was in the detention center alone began crying. I learned she had been separated from an aunt at the border . . . as she cried in the middle of the interview, the attorney working with her took the girl by the hand and walked over to a teen detainee who was holding a two-year old. It turned out that the teen girl—who was not a mother or a relative—had been comforting the toddler and six-year-old for days out of a sense of sympathy.[19]

In an interview with *Slate* magazine, Ong Hing described the deplorable conditions of the Clint facility. On the day he visited, 350 children were held in cramped rooms with 20 to 50 children per room. Most of the children he spoke with had been separated from their parents and detained for more than twelve days, some up to twenty days. He found the younger children unbathed, with dirty hair, and wearing dirty clothes, and some children lacking socks. "I came to realize that the younger children were dirtier than the older children," he said, "because the smaller ones were hesitant to bathe by themselves; there was also no one who helped them wash their clothes." He interviewed a sick child who had not seen a doctor and girls who reported feeling unsafe to use the bathroom. The children told him they were hungry and did not have enough food to eat. "One of the most striking things I witnessed was how toddlers are left to care for themselves—including a two-year-old."[20]

During the Trump administration, thousands of children were held in overcrowded and unsanitary cages after forcible separation from their parents. Several children died in federal custody. After years of legal challenges, in May 2022, the Center for Human Rights and Constitutional Law reached a settlement with the US Border Patrol to provide humane conditions of detention and not to separate children from their parents.[21]

When the Plantation Overseers Came for Maritza

In the past and the present, Indigenous lands that were usurped by plantations were focal points of civil protest and state violence in Guatemala.[22] Large landowners had long relied on state repression to keep their ill-gotten lands, along with the Indigenous laborers living in serf-like conditions. The army utilized this conflict from the Cold War to the present to maintain political power, while plantation owners used the doctrine of national security and anticommunist ideology to eliminate all dissent and any land rights organizing. Indeed, the Guatemalan truth commission identified the long-standing historic unequal distribution of land and structural discrimination against the Maya as root causes of the conflict.[23]

This alliance between local plantation owners and the army led to selective violence against rural leaders, beginning with forced disappearances and assassinations. Land rights leaders, union organizers, literacy teachers, catechists, priests, nuns, doctors, nurses, and teachers were the first to be targeted. Later, any Maya leader who spoke Spanish was eliminated—thus limiting the ability of rural Maya (and especially rural Maya women) to seek justice. As one K'ekchi' Maya massacre survivor told me, "After they killed my son, there was no one left to speak for me." This selective violence was followed with massive, systematic violence that was a planned genocide.[24]

This violence was not only committed by army soldiers; it was also committed by local military commissioners and members of the army-controlled civil patrols, as well as plantation managers and overseers who had always seen Indigenous women as property—an attitude that dates not only to the colonial era but also to the late eighteenth and early nineteenth centuries when German immigrants were given large areas of land, along with its Indigenous inhabitants as serfs to perform free labor.[25] In San Andrés Sajcabajá, survivors recounted to me how Don Polo, a large landowner and local military commissioner, would mount his horse and go to the paths that Indigenous women had to use to get water. He would grab them and take them away on his horse to rape them in the woods. While conducting research there in 1997, I gained access to Don Polo for an interview. Before I could ask any questions, he said, "These women are all mistaken. I was not here then. Look, I have a doctor's note." He dug through a drawer in his desk and produced a small, signed note that read (absurdly): "Señor Polo was hospitalized for eye surgery in Guatemala City from 1981 to 1983." He said to me, "This is here in ink and signed by a doctor. All they have are their words that have no value."

The Mam Maya from the Todos Santos region were a strategic target for the army because of the historic relationship between them and Catholic Action colonization projects in northern Ixcán communities. Indeed, Todos Santeros and other Mam Maya from the region who had migrated to Ixcán were among the first killed by the army.[26] Though initially supported by the government in the late 1960s as a way to mollify rural protest over the usurpation of ancestral lands by gifting faraway parcels, by the 1980s, these colonization projects had become successful cooperatives and demonstrated the possibilities of economic success for peasants working collectively.[27] This threatened the seasonal labor supply of large coffee plantations that relied on peasant poverty to provide a cheap labor pool. For the military regime, any collective organization was seen as a threat. Thus the Mam of the Todos Santos region and in Ixcán cooperatives suffered repression. Moreover, the violence against the cooperatives gave the large plantations carte blanche in their labor practices during and after the genocide.

The misery of extreme poverty is what makes Indigenous women so vulnerable to exploitation on plantations. In the Huehuetenango region, 64 percent of inhabitants suffer chronic and severe malnutrition. Eighty of 100 children are underweight, suffer low growth for their age, and exhibit a generalized failure to thrive due to chronic malnutrition. Those who become ill are hard pressed to access medical services; there are no hospitals in rural communities, and there is only one doctor for every 3,761 inhabitants.[28] To ensure public health, a minimum of 3 general practitioners per 1,000 population is considered at the bottom of the baseline.[29] Thus ten times the number of doctors would be needed to meet the most basic public health standards in Huehuetenango.

Just as the male head of household makes all decisions and his offspring must abide and enforce decisions, the plantation overseer and his henchmen determine all that happens in the life of workers on the plantations, including where they work, what their work entails, how long they work, what they are paid, where they sleep, what they eat, and what they owe the plantation for room and board. This means that girls and women, who already have less value and lower status, are paid less than men and have fewer rights than men. It also means that a girl or a woman must obey the orders of the overseer and his henchmen, just as she is required to obey the patriarch of her family. Any deviation from the rules is subject to punishment. Corporal punishment and withholding of food are the norm in families and on plantations. The use of corporal punishment against women and girls has been documented on plantations as well as in factories in Guatemala.[30]

Maritza was born in a village high in the mountains of Huehuetenango a few years before the peace accords were signed in 1996.[31] A monolingual Mam speaker, she was never allowed to go to school and is illiterate. She has been doing domestic chores since her earliest memories. Her parents sent her to work as a day laborer on a finca when she was 15. She met her husband, Pedro, at the finca. Pedro had been allowed to go to primary school for two years. He could not read or write, but he could speak a little Spanish. Together they decided to migrate to work on a coffee plantation where the owner would allow them to live in a shack and give them a small amount of land to cultivate their own food. Though both Pedro and Maritza were still in their teens, they saw this migration as an opportunity to have a family, and they had three children in as many years.

As an adult, Maritza was responsible for managing all household chores as well as working in the fields where she was paid 35 quetzales per eleven-hour workday. That is US$4.49 per day, the equivalent of 41 cents per hour. Even in Guatemala, this is not a living wage; rather it is the wage of misery. In April 2015, the basic food basket for a family of four was 3,697 quetzales (US$482) per month (just for food). If Maritza was working six days a week, she earned just

840 quetzales (if they actually paid her what she was owed). Those 840 quetzales (US$110) represent just 22 percent of the Guatemalan government's calculation of the minimum income necessary to obtain sufficient caloric intake for a family of four to escape hunger.[32] This is not the basic food basket, which includes medical care, education, transportation, and housing, which is currently 6,747 quetzales (US$887) per month to live above the poverty line—eight times the wage Maritza receives. Plantation owners will suggest that they provide housing for their workers and thus pay them fairly. They fail to mention that they charge their workers for the housing, which is below substandard. I visited one plantation where the workers slept in a former (and unimproved) chicken coop for which rent was discounted from their earnings.

Juan and Maritza and their children all worked on the coffee plantation. Their combined earnings totaled less than half the cost of a food basket for a family of four. One day in 2015, her husband did not return from the fields. Even in postwar Guatemala, the levels of violence are so great that she assumed he had been killed. In her husband's absence, Maritza and her children were vulnerable to the whims of the overseer and his corporals. While she was the de facto head of household, she had no recourse to protect her son or daughters. Maritza had no recourse to protection when the henchmen arrived looking for her husband after he disappeared. This was how she learned that he had fled in fear for his life.

When four men from the plantation came looking for her husband, Maritza was pregnant, alone with two small children, and had no one to protect her. There was nothing she could do to stop the unlawful search of her home by these violent men, nor could she intervene to stop the damage they caused to her few precious possessions. It was only when some neighbors arrived that these men stopped harassing and groping her. There was nowhere for her to go to make a legal complaint or seek justice.

A few days later, the henchmen attacked Maritza and her son with impunity, just as the plantation henchmen had previously invaded and searched her home. The henchmen beat Maritza and her son. They ripped Maritza's huipil, tore at her clothing, and groped her. Then the plantation goons tied Maritza and her son to trees. They beat Maritza until she lost consciousness. The attack itself is evocative of army and civil patrol violence wherein a tree is not just a tree but rather a site to be utilized for punishment, torture, and example. Violence becomes a spectacle to punish and discipline not just the victim, but the entire community by proxy.[33]

This attack against Maritza is also reminiscent of the mass violence carried out against Indigenous women during the genocide and in its aftermath. Many Maya women were gang-raped and silenced by shame and custom. With few exceptions, the perpetrators of these crimes have never been brought to justice. The patterns or practice of gender violence and mass rape established in the past by war criminals continue to be carried out against Indigenous women by men who hold power over them.[34]

Neighbors found Maritza and her son tied to trees when they were walking to tend their fields in the early morning hours. The neighbors freed Maritza and her son. Seeing their multiple injuries, they immediately took them to a medical clinic. Maritza was given a superficial medical exam and medication for pain and sent home. She was not hospitalized. The medical report simply notes multiple lacerations and contusions. There is no recommendation for medical or psychological follow-up. There is no referral to police or prosecutors.

Moreover, given Maritza's condition after the attack, the medical clinic personnel should have conducted a gynecological exam consistent with a rape kit. Indeed, if a semiconscious non-Maya urban woman was taken to a medical clinic in Guatemala City, even if she did not state she had been raped, the medical personnel would have conducted at least an external examination because the exam is not only for treatment but also for the collection of evidence. In addition, the examining physician and/or nurse should have interviewed her about the attack and asked her directly if she had been raped. The police and the prosecutor should have been called in as soon as Maritza presented herself at the clinic. Here the system failed Maritza yet again. No one ever asked her if she had been raped. No one called the police or the Prosecutor's Office to report her assault.

As the women's rights advocate Carolina Escobar Sarti explained to me, if a woman has visible marks from physical or sexual aggression, medical personnel should conduct a complete exam using a rape kit and send the results to the INACIF as forensic evidence. "But," Carolina explained, "this is in theory. The health system is poor, social imaginaries continue to normalize sexual violence on the bodies of girls and women, and language is a barrier as well."[35] Norma Cruz, founder of the Survivors Foundation, told me that only INACIF can carry out a legal rape kit exam—which means that rape victims must go to the morgue. Further, even if the victim does not state that she is raped, the doctors are required by law to contact the Prosecutor's Office. At the same time, failure to alert the prosecutor of a possible rape is a criminal violation with punishment ranging from loss of the right to practice medicine to a jail sentence and/or monetary fine. A feminist Guatemalan lawyer told me that the law requires doctors to conduct a full rape exam. "Imagine if the victim was unconscious or unable to speak," she explained. "These doctors should be denounced for negligence and racism." She offered to begin a legal process. She also told me about the case of Juana Méndez Rodríguez.

In January 2007, police detained Juana Méndez Rodríguez for not denouncing her neighbors' opium poppy crops. Against her will, they held Juana in jail as a material witness in the case. While detained, she was gang-raped and beaten by police, who then forced her to parade naked through the Nebaj police station. There they forced her to shower, thereby washing away the evidence of the sexual assault while being further humiliated as she was forced to shower in front of other detainees.[36]

A 2005 study indicated that 75 percent of women in detention were subjected to abuses and sexual assault by police. Further, 43 percent of the victims denounced their abuse in court, but only one case was investigated by the Prosecutor's Office.[37] The case of Juana Méndez Rodríguez was the first case of police sexual assault to be heard by a tribunal. The court's decision was important because it not only found the officers guilty but also recognized rape by police officials as a form of torture. The expert testimony also pointed to significant insufficiencies in medical provision of services to rape victims. Dr. Isaías Juárez, former director of the regional hospital in Nebaj, testified that he had examined Juana the day after the attack. He testified that he had no knowledge of protocols for rape victims. Further, he testified that the first time he ever conducted a gynecological exam was when he examined Juana Méndez Rodríguez. In his medical report, he concluded that he had found no evidence of rape.[38] During the court hearing, local Ixil Maya women marched carrying placards that read, "Doña Juana, su verdad es mi verdad" (Doña Juana, your truth is my truth) and "Mi cuerpo es mío. No se toca. No se viola. No se mata" (My body is mine. Don't touch it. Don't rape it. Don't kill it).[39]

In the end, both officers were dismissed from their positions in the National Civilian Police. Importantly, the court found them guilty of rape and abuse of authority.[40] Antonio Rutilio Matías López is serving a jail sentence, but Nery Osberto Aldana Rodríguez fled and remains a fugitive. The gang rape and the public humiliation Juana suffered in the police station, as well as the egregious violation of medical standards by Dr. Juárez, call into question the competency of police and medical personnel in their professional obligations to support rape victims and collect evidence to prosecute perpetrators. Dr. Juárez has not been charged with any criminal violation, nor has he been placed under any type of administrative review or professional proceeding.

While a clinic failing to collect this type of evidence and failing to notify the police and the Prosecutor's Office in Guatemala is technically in violation of the law, few clinics are charged, and the farther one is from the capital city, the farther one is from the possibility of justice. In these two cases, this distance from justice is further compounded by Juana's and Maritza's monolingual, rural Maya status.

Against all odds, Juana found her voice and opened political space for other women to publicly protest and denounce the crimes perpetrated against them. Maritza, like most Indigenous rape victims, is also a victim of the silencing of Maya women.[41] They are actively discouraged from discussing the details of assaults and attacks on their physical integrity by their communities, as well as by medical and judicial personnel who should be protecting them. Maritza and Juana are both victims of the justice system that fails to provide them with security and equal protection before the law. Maritza is also a victim of the men who attacked her and the plantation system that protects them.

Maritza fled Guatemala because she had no safe place to seek refuge. She would have continued to be under threat as an Indigenous woman who fled plantation violence, which makes her suspect in a country where the assumption is always one of victim precipitation—that is, that the victim is responsible for her victimization. She would be viewed as suspicious, a potential troublemaker or maybe a union or land rights organizer. This is especially the case in isolated, closed corporate communities like the plantation where Maritza worked. Indigenous women and girls stand little chance of any legal protection from plantation overseer and henchmen abuse, violence, and torture. Much as those who fled slave plantations were kept on lists, Indigenous workers who flee plantation abuse and sexual violence are followed and/or blacklisted.

For most women, the police are a source of danger, not protection. A European Union survey showed that the police had raped more than a third of women who went to them to report a crime.[42] The human rights community has attempted to change that violent police culture through training and new policies, but their attempts have most often been met with open scorn and derision. The police seem to feel entitled to assault women.

Profiling the Killing of Women in Guatemala

What types of criminal profiles can we develop to understand the killing of women in Guatemala? While the data provided by the police and prosecutors are inadequate in many ways, we can begin to develop new ways of understanding feminicide by reviewing the data, analyses, and conclusions of police and prosecutors regarding the killing of women over time. When Claudina Isabel was killed in 2005, the Guatemalan police, based on their superficial registration of individual murders of women, classified the "cause" as follows: 21 percent of female homicide victims involved gangs; 21 percent had personal problems; 17 percent had problems with passion; 10 percent were killed during a robbery; 9 percent were involved in drug trafficking; 5 percent died when they were raped; 4 percent died in cross fire; and the remaining 13 percent are grouped together as victims of carjacking, suicide, or domestic violence leading to murder.[43]

Given the ease with which the police chose not to investigate Claudina Isabel's murder based on their presumptive finding that she was a gang member, I wonder how they determined that 21 percent of these women were involved with gangs. As for personal problems, who doesn't have some? But personal problems do not a murder victim make. Moving on to problems with passion, even if the police mean a crime of passion (which is a crime of hate in disguise, just as stalking is not romantic), in their lexicon it is the murder

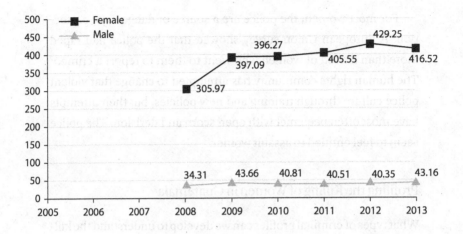

FIGURE 2. Intrafamily violence in Guatemala, 2008–2013. Courtesy of Dorian Caal.

victim who had passion problems. So the police blame the victim for her killer not being able to control his "passion"? The drug trafficking and cross-fire categories are equally dubious given the lack of crime scene control and the poor record of even maintaining custody of bullets, much less conducting a thorough ballistics analysis along with a coordinated forensic study of the bullet's trajectory from entry to exit. Given that only an autopsy can determine the type of sexual assault to which a woman has been subjected and the fact that an examination for rape is not a standard protocol for murder victims at the Guatemala City morgue, the rape category reads like an after-thought.

Returning to the macro of counting feminicide victims, how do the police and forensic medical examiners classify the homicides? The general randomness (or shall we say, fiction) of the categories of victims is almost immaterial once we look at the actual contents claimed by the police. For example, women who were victims of domestic violence leading to murder are mixed in with those who died in a carjacking and those who committed suicide. All we know then is that they are less than 13 percent of victims, according to the police.[44] This is striking because international research on the killing of women indicates that the murder of women by intimate partners accounts for 37 to 49 percent of all female homicides.[45] It is highly unlikely and statistically improbable that Guatemala would have a low rate of intimate partner murders of women when the overall killing of women is skyrocketing across the country. Indeed, the Guatemalan rapper Rebeca Lane has called attention to intimate partner violence: "We are being killed by our fathers, brothers, stepfathers, the very people who are supposed to care for us."[46]

Lane's assertion is supported by facts. In his analysis of Guatemalan government data on intrafamily violence (violence against women), the statistician Dorian Caal observes that both intrafamily violence and sexual violence have steadily increased since 2009. Further, he suspects that even though these numbers are high, the real numbers of women victims of violence in the private sphere are higher than reported, due to women not reporting out of fear of retaliation and additional abuse.[47] I would add that many women do not report due to fear of assault and rape at the hands of police.

4 *#TengoMiedo (#IAmAfraid)*

Lidia's Story

Guatemalan women and children of all classes are subjected to violence and abuse within intimate and family relationships because perpetrators know that their victims are unable to defend themselves or receive government protection. Abusers view women and children as property and inflict violence and harm on them because of their status in these relationships. While middle- and upper-class status confers many social and economic benefits, it does not guarantee a life free of gender violence.

Before Lidia and her husband were married,[1] during courtship, he appeared to be the solution to any financial worries she might have had prior to marriage because he was a lawyer with wealth and prestige. However, he used this wealth and prestige to further dominate Lidia and force her to do his bidding. He did not see her as an equal partner in their marriage, or in society. In this, his position was in keeping with the majority of men in Guatemala. He was among the 58 percent of Guatemalan men who believe they have the right to use physical violence against their spouse.[2]

Lidia was the property of her husband, who felt free to verbally abuse and physically assault her. He was always angry and issuing mandates about mundane household activities, from the temperature of breakfast to the order of grocery list items and the payment of utility bills. To emphasize his orders to Lidia, he would grab her by the hair, push her up against the wall, and hold her by the neck—to be sure she paid the phone bill or picked up his dry cleaning. She was terrified. He would also terrorize her by driving at dangerous speeds. In a show of macho power, he included Lucía, their two-year-old daughter, in this abuse by dangerously placing her in the front seat of the car without a seatbelt or car seat and driving at high speeds, leaving Lucía in tears and Lidia silenced with terror. He was able to behave in this way because he had no fear of retribution or legal sanction.

Here again the dynamic of vulnerability and abuse is repeated, from the hierarchy of the family to citizen interactions with the judicial system to the blur between legal and extralegal or clandestine structures. The conflation of men's beliefs in a husband's right to assault his wife and lack of legal access for women reinforces Lidia's isolation. Neither Lidia nor her daughter has any recourse to protection. Lidia's husband viewed Lidia as his property by virtue of his role as the patriarch in the family and utilized his power to remind her of her inferior position, even after he had taken up with another woman and divorced Lidia.

Violence Affects All Women and Children

The year before Lidia fled Guatemala City, 759 women and girls were killed—a 7 percent increase over the number of women killed in 2012. And the women were killed with brutality: 522 were killed by bullets, 70 were stabbed to death, 156 were asphyxiated, and 11 died from decapitation or dismemberment. Although the government established special new courts in 2008 to investigate, less than 10 percent of the 2012 killings of women were investigated and resolved.[3]

Indeed, after he had abandoned his family, Lidia's husband would threaten Lidia and demand to see their daughter. Following their divorce, he would show up unannounced, in violation of their custody agreement, and demand access to Lucía. Fearing his powerful legal friends, Lidia would reluctantly allow him to take Lucía for the day. When he would drop off Lucía at the end of the day, she often had bruises on her face, a split lip, or bruised bumps on her head. Lucía would cry and scream that she did not want to leave with her father. On one occasion, when he left her at the door at the end of the day, two-year-old Lucía was trembling, teeth chattering, with blue lips, her clothes soaking wet, and her hands freezing cold (this in the land of eternal spring with an average temperature of 72 degrees Fahrenheit). He claimed Lucía had vomited in the morning from motion sickness. Then he rinsed her and her clothes in cold water, then kept her in those clothes for the entire day. Inexplicably, he was running the air-conditioner in the car, which made her even colder. Lidia became gravely concerned for Lucía's safety.

At the same time, whenever he appeared at Lidia's, he would threaten her, hit her, and hold her against the wall by the neck. Emboldened by her powerlessness, each time he would laugh and remind her, "They can't do anything." Lidia hired a lawyer, who filed a restraining order with a local judge and apprised the police of Lidia's situation. Lidia received a copy of the restraining order— a piece of paper. Stamped and duly signed. This paper did not stop her ex-husband from showing up at her house unannounced at all hours of the day and night.

Lidia recalls, "I would awaken to him pounding on my door, scratching at my windows. I would call the police telling them, 'He is here. He is yelling and pounding on the door, trying to get into my house. He is trying to break into my home.' The police would not arrive. I would call again and again. Each time he came to my house, I would call the police. When they did arrive, they would laugh at me.

The police would make fun of me as if it was all a big joke. That is why he kept coming back. He knew they would do nothing."

And here, again, we have a case of a lawyer and a judge, however well meaning, misapplying the Femicide Law because they only sought the restraining order through the old intrafamily violence code. They never sought charges against a man who felt it was his right to torture his former wife and abuse their daughter. Every time Lidia left her home to go to work or to the store or to visit her family, she feared an attack by her ex-husband.

For Lidia, an educated, upper-middle-class, urban woman, the restraining order is as vacuous as it is for marginalized rural women. It is an archived document counted by the government that turns Lidia, Magda, and other women into statistics. It is a testament in the present and the future to the grave violence to which Guatemalan women of the early twenty-first century are subjected. No one was instructed to protect Lidia or her daughter, Lucía. And in Lidia's particular situation, the restraining order has serious consequences for her because her ex-husband is a powerful, wealthy lawyer. This means that he probably knew about the restraining order before she had it in her hand.

When Lidia received the restraining order, she left the court with that piece of paper but with no safe place to take her daughter. There is no government program to assist women and children to access safe housing and shelter to hide from abuse. Though upper middle class, Lidia had no family to support her against her powerful ex-husband. So here again the restraining order is really only useful when the government of Guatemala prepares its statistics on its protection of the rights of women and children and adds Lidia's restraining order to its list of accomplishments. But in real life, in Lidia's life, and in Lucía's life (as in Magda's life), the restraining order is meaningless.

Indeed, gender-based violence is about power and dominance. Having no safe place to live with Lucía, Lidia fled to the United States in search of safety and freedom for herself and her daughter. But her ex-husband has resources, and he is an angry man who does not want to see his dominance thwarted, especially by a woman he abandoned and later divorced. He is a lawyer and he knows lawyers. Citing the Hague Convention, he petitioned in the United States for the return of Lucía to his custody in Guatemala, arguing that Lidia had abducted Lucía. His legal petition was an extreme example of his unwillingness to give up his power over Lidia. By filing the lawsuit, he terrorizes Lidia with the uncertainty of the outcome, the fear she will never see her daughter again, and the danger to which Lucía will be subjected in Guatemala (that of her father as well as the ambient violence), and he also reminds her that the power of his wealth and reach is so great he can still keep her awake at night with worry, that he can still get her—even in the United States. The petition for Lucía's return to Guatemala is terrifying because it reminds Lidia of the Guatemalan legal system where her ex-husband is powerful and she has no equal access. It reminds her that the Guatemalan legal system did not protect her and that she has nowhere to go for protection. She wonders if she should move farther north to Canada. She wants to believe that safety and justice are within reach, but she worries through the multiple hearings of this petition and all the legal costs. Quite reasonably, she fears for her life and Lucía's life.

The continuum of gender violence from the past to the present includes the particular ways that traditional cultural practices become instruments of repression and how these instruments of repression continue to mark all levels of Guatemalan society. Guatemala has one of the highest female homicide rates in the world. It has a history of violent conflict and is a place where successive modern civilian governments remain dominated by the military and are unable to protect citizens from harm at the hands of gangs, organized crime, and drug traffickers. Women and children are similarly unable to receive protection from intimate partner violence and family violence. This is especially the case for a woman like Lidia who suffers a loss of social, economic, and political power in her divorce from her ex-husband who maintains his social and political power, and prestige. No charges have ever been brought against him. Lidia and Lucía are victims of impunity.

Impunity and State Inaction

The national Prosecutor's Office has a special prosecutor for crimes against women. As we sought justice for Claudina Isabel, this prosecutor stated on several occasions that there is no specific cause for violence against women because all violence in Guatemala has increased. Therefore, according to the prosecutor charged with resolving the murders of women, the astronomical rise in the killing of women is only incidental to this general increase. Much of civil society, drawing from newspaper articles, blames gangs, serial killers, and drug traffickers for the high levels of interpersonal violence in Guatemala. Some congressional deputies with ties to military political parties argue that the homicide rate justifies increased military presence to secure neighborhoods: it is not uncommon to see several dozen heavily armed police and soldiers patrolling neighborhoods together (in direct violation of the 1996 peace accords). Still other congressional deputies believe the homicide rate can be explained by a combination of organized crime and drug traffickers using the murders as a distraction. They point to the fact that these murders are happening at a time when the redefinition of the army and public security is being debated. They further argue that this violence is destabilizing and in the interest of what many have come to refer to in Guatemala as "parallel powers."[4]

The United Nations also connects the impunity of the brutal assassination of women in the post–Peace Accord era with the existence of parallel powers holding the recourse to violence that increases their power and a state with no political will to stop them. Indeed, these parallel powers are so strong that the International Commission against Impunity was established by the United Nations and the Guatemalan Congress with the hope of reining in these powers through investigation and prosecution. CICIG was established through an agreement first signed by the United Nations and the Government of Guatemala in 2006 that was subsequently ratified by the Congress of Guatemala in August of 2007.[5] This was no small feat. Previous efforts had been thwarted by the Guatemalan Congress on the grounds that such investigative bodies violated the sovereignty of Guatemala. Ironically, the first permutation of CICIG was voted down by Congress on grounds of sovereignty just days before the same Congress voted in favor of the Central America Free Trade Agreement (CAFTA)—which effectively suborns the Constitution of Guatemala to CAFTA.

Though lacking the teeth of the original Commission which would have had prosecutorial power, CICIG was established as "an independent, international body designed to support the Public Prosecutor's Office (MP), the National Civilian Police (PNC) and other State institutions in the investigation of crimes committed by members of illegal security forces and clandestine security structures." CICIG was charged with assisting in the investigation and development of criminal prosecutions of illegal security groups and clandestine security structures with the goal of disbanding them. The police and the penitentiary system were among the key institutions identified as priority targets for CICIG investigations when it began its mandate in 2007.[6]

A core belief of the CICIG process is that by supporting Guatemalan agencies in the investigation and prosecution of clandestine, illegal groups, the judicial system is also strengthened and empowered to carry forth prosecutorial efforts against illegal, clandestine groups. Since its initial authorization for two years in 2007, its mandate was renewed in 2009, 2011, 2013, 2015, and again in 2017. CICIG's last mandate expired in September 2019 and was not renewed by then-president Jimmy Morales, who was himself under investigation.[7]

CICIG's mandate had three core goals: (1) investigate clandestine groups that "affect the fundamental human rights of the citizens of Guatemala" and identify clandestine structures as well as their activities, operational strategies, financing, and their links to other groups, including government offices and government officials; (2) assist the government of Guatemala to "disband these clandestine security structures and illegal security groups" and promote the investigation, prosecution, and sanction of group members responsible for criminal activities; and (3) make recommendations to the government of Guatemala regarding necessary governmental reforms to eliminate current clandestine groups and prevent the resurgence of these and other clandestine security structures and illegal security forces.[8]

The work of CICIG was daunting for the investigators because of the ways in which former and current military networks have restructured and entrenched themselves in Guatemala in a complex web of organized crime, drug trafficking, and gangs each with links to different police and army units as well as political parties. Gangs also have ties to the police and can in fact be hunted by the police if they have not paid their quota to the police or have simply become too big a liability after having carried out illicit activities for the police. Much in the same way, gangs have ties to drug traffickers and organized crime, which, in turn, also have ties to the military and police.

In his work as CICIG Commissioner (2013–19), Ivan Velásquez and his team accompanied and strengthened local investigative and prosecutorial powers. They developed an in-depth analysis of the composition and functioning of clandestine groups in Guatemala. Velásquez identifies illegal and clandestine groups (Cuerpos Ilegales y Aparatos Clandestinos de Seguridad [CIACS]) as networks of political power that join together to carry out political and economic activities that move between the licit and the illicit.[9] Importantly, he also points out that both legal and illegal activities of CIACS are carried out with some level of involvement of government authorities. In sum, these activities amount to complex criminal enterprises that are supported by political and economic networks with deep ties to the legal political hierarchy.[10]

CIACS have depth and breadth of experience in politics and business. They are involved in licit and illicit political processes and commerce. They carry out illicit economic transactions. They exercise political control to generate profitable businesses. The combination of political and economic activities, both legal and illegal, generates a rapid rise in a social hierarchy empowering individuals and groups who form a part of the operations of the CIACS.

CIACS consolidate power through the de-ideologization of the political process on the one hand and illicit enrichment on the other. They do not necessarily subvert the constitutional order because they seek to use it as a tool for their own ends. At the same time, they have an unscrupulous disregard for laws and regulations. Because they play inside and outside the system, they are able to disrupt, stall, and inhibit legal, administrative, and judicial processes. CIACS increase illicit wealth in society through their improper use of power, undue influence, and economic force. Democratic processes are subverted by the existence, actions, and power of the CIACS. The oligarchy, however, maintains its power and functions in tandem with these parallel powers sustained by corruption and impunity.

Violence, Corruption, and Migration

Violence and corruption are the main drivers of migration from Guatemala.[11] From the swift detention and deportation of refugees under the Obama administration to the cruel separation of children from their mothers and the massive border wall building under Trump to the Biden administration's claims to address the root problems of migration, ever-increasing numbers of Guatemalan asylum seekers risk their lives each day to reach the US border. From Obama to Trump to Biden, the United States has failed to address the root causes of migration. It has simultaneously militarized the US border and the borderlands of Mexico and Central America by using proxy forces. The March 2021 deployment of 10,000 Mexican troops on the México-Guatemala border, 1,500 Guatemalan troops on its border with Honduras, and a "surge" of 7,000 troops within Honduras did not stop migration or rein in violence. US support for armed squads to face down Central American civilians is a known path to catastrophe—from the forced disappearances and massacres of the 1980s to contemporary violence wreaking havoc on the daily life of Central Americans.

One week after the United States ratified an agreement for $530,000 in US assistance to Guatemalan president Alejandro Giammattei's Presidential Commission against Corruption, Giammattei suspended Guatemalan rights to freedom of assembly in five departments near the Honduran border. Following a similar decree in January 2021, Guatemalan police and army soldiers attacked a group of Honduran families with tear gas and batons at a border checkpoint. On March 30, 2021, a Mexican soldier killed a Guatemalan at a border checkpoint. This killing followed on the heels of the repatriation of thirteen Guatemalans killed and burned by Mexican police in the Mexican state of Tamaulipas near the US border.

Given Giammattei's history, it is not surprising that the March 2021 contribution to his commission did not slow the exodus of Guatemalans or make a dent in the struggle against corruption. In 2010, Giammattei was arrested for his role as national prison director in the 2006 Pavon prison massacre—categorized as a series of planned extrajudicial executions by CICIG. After charges were dropped, Giammattei ran for president, promoting the massacre as his "successful" retaking of the prison. Giammattei won his fourth campaign for president in 2019 after the leading candidate, former attorney general and anticorruption crusader, Thelma Aldana, was driven into exile. In February 2021, Aldana posted, "I am afraid of going back to Guatemala and being killed," with the hashtag #TengoMiedo (#IAmAfraid)—the Guatemalan Twitter campaign against gender violence. Granted political asylum in the United States, Aldana joined her predecessor in exile, former attorney general Claudia Paz y Paz, who led successful anticorruption cases with CICIG, in addition to securing convictions of army officers involved in the genocide of the 1980s. Aldana was replaced by Giammattei's right-hand woman, Consuelo Porras, who has taken a hard line in disarticulating the anticorruption cases and attacking anticorruption prosecutors and judges.[12] Corruption and threats of violence have driven twenty-eight Guatemalan anticorruption justice operators to seek exile in Mexico, Spain, and the United States since 2018 when Jimmy Morales banned CICIG Commissioner Velásquez from entering Guatemala.[13]

Erika Aifán, a judge on Guatemala's high-risk court, had always faced threats to her life and career. The threats intensified as she began to hear a case implicating President Giammattei as the recipient of a rug stuffed with cash. A protected witness in the corruption case accused Giammattei of the extensive negotiation of bribes for campaign contributions. Aifán told the *New Yorker* that the Guatemalan government was pressuring her to reveal the identity of the protected witness, whose name she kept in her safe. She had explosive testimony that detailed the government's efforts to "eliminate witnesses and victims." Whereas Paz y Paz and Aldana had led valiant efforts as attorneys general to combat corruption and support anticorruption judges and prosecutors, Giammattei's appointee, Consuelo Porras, has used the power of the attorney general's office to obstruct anticorruption cases, including filing two complaints against Aifán seeking to strip her of judicial immunity from prosecution. In tandem, the Orwellian Foundation Against Terrorism (a genocide denial disinformation front for former and current military officers claiming to fight terrorism) has also filed a case against Aifán. Meanwhile, the first hearings in Aifán's appeals were held under cloak of secrecy because the presiding judge denied Aifán's requests for a public hearing. If her case had made it to the Supreme Court for review, it would have been decided by thirteen judges—seven of whom were defendants in one of the corruption cases in Aifán's court. Recently exiled, she recounted to the *New Yorker,* "I have been followed by unmarked cars. I have been filmed and recorded, and the videos have been posted on social media."[14] On March 21, in a Twitter video post from Washington, DC, Aifán explained she was resigning "because I can't rely on sufficient guarantees for my own personal and physical protection nor for the possibility of defending myself with due process."[15]

Whether justice operators seeking to prosecute corruption or regular citizens trying to take a bus to work without having to pay a "tax" to the local gang, rule of law is essential for Guatemalan society to give its citizens a measure of security. Corruption drives legal and illegal migration because it collapses public space and civic possibility. Migration from Guatemala went down 35 percent during CICIG's first year of anticorruption work in Guatemala. For five years, the number of Guatemalans apprehended at the US border continued to drop.[16] CICIG's successes are a model for the region to follow to fight against corruption and slow the exodus of citizens.

While disliked by the powerful and the corrupt, CICIG had a 70 percent approval rating in Guatemala in 2017. Working with Guatemalan prosecutors, CICIG dismantled more than 70 criminal networks, investigated and prosecuted 100 high-impact cases, brought 600 suspects to trial, and convicted 400. (That is a 66 percent prosecution rate for CICIG compared to the MP's 2 percent homicide prosecution rate.)[17] CICIG prosecutions supported Guatemalan prosecutors and made it possible for regular citizens to access justice. As the powerful and corrupt ramped up unrelenting attacks on CICIG and the Trump administration was silent, then-president Jimmy Morales, who was himself under investigation and had an approval rating below 20 percent, did not renew CICIG's mandate in 2019, and a record 264,168 Guatemalans were caught on the US-Mexico border.[18]

Giammattei claims Guatemala no longer needs an international presence for prosecutors to safely do their jobs. But if this were true, the two top corruption fighters, Aldana and Paz y Paz, would not be in exile and the current attorney general would not be using the power of her office to file specious charges against the very prosecutor's unit meant to investigate corruption. In 2022, anticorruption crusader and elected judge, Gloria Porras, was denied her seat on the Constitutional Court by a murky legal challenge stripping the court of its independence and leaving judges vulnerable to the whims of the powerful.

Giammattei's anticorruption commission is the latest in a long trail of presidential Ponzi schemes in Guatemala. Former president Otto Pérez Molina, a former general, utilized the office of the presidency to establish his own import tax system, called La Línea, the Line. The $120 million stolen from customs coffers was part of the $535 million lost to corruption in 2015. The indictment of Pérez Molina and other high-ranking officials revealed the complex arrangements that tie politicians to security structures, cartels, organized crime, and the private sector.[19]

The Biden administration's late 2021 policy of private sector investment in Guatemala to stem migration is counterproductive and feeds the very structures that push migration.[20] Guatemalans overwhelmingly supported CICIG because it offered a glimpse of how rule of law could break the chokehold of grifters and clandestine organizations on the state. While Guatemalan migration spiked during the first two years of Pérez Molina's crooked regime, the number of Guatemalans at our southern border decreased by 29 percent when he was arrested on corruption charges in 2015.[21] Not surprisingly, the homicide rate also affects migration. The Dialogue reports that a 1 percent rise in homicides in Guatemala coincides with a 100 percent increase in migration from Guatemala.[22]

The Targeting of Women

The Inter-American Commission for Human Rights (IACHR) concluded that the assassinations of women are meant to signal to women to watch out and return to the private sphere of the home and their familial duties. As women have taken on more public roles and are viewed as competing with men, they are told to abandon the public arena and give up on civic participation. While working on a feminicide case, one investigator told me that he had commented to a director at the Guatemala City morgue, "Isn't it terrible, all these young women being killed?" The director, responsible for overseeing all autopsies of feminicide victims, snorted back, "What do they expect? Taking on the roles of men, they have it coming."

Guatemalan feminicide means that women cannot safely walk alone at night anywhere in the country. Moreover, as IACHR Rapporteur Susan Villarán has reaffirmed, the classification by police of the killing of women as crimes of passion is not based on investigation. Rather it is based on discriminating against women, blaming the victim, and revictimizing the families of victims by blaming the victim for being unfaithful, jealous, dishonest, and/or damaging the honor of the man.[23] This IACHR determination is supported by Amnesty International, which has concluded that murders classified as "crimes of passion" are never investigated.[24] The police labeling of murdered young men as gang members and of murdered young women as prostitutes obfuscates the connections between social cleansing and feminicide. While the link between the killing of women and social cleansing may not be immediately visible given that only 2 percent of women murdered have been known prostitutes, my journey through the land of pale hands has led me to believe that the high incidence of the killing of women is cynically used to justify social cleansing of poor young men who are blamed as supposed "gang members" for what is actually feminicide. Given the very low homicide prosecution rates, it is unsurprising that, in practice, there are no legal consequences for killing people who are socially undesirable in Guatemala.

For example, former general Otto Pérez Molina's 2011 presidential bid was grounded in his *mano dura* (strong hand) stance against crime and gangs. During his actual presidency, violence in Guatemala in general, and the killing of women in particular, continued to increase in tandem with the expansion of gangs, drug trafficking, organized crime, and government corruption. My analysis of Guatemalan National Police crime data, Guatemalan Prosecutor's Office annual data, and World Health Organization data on crime in Guatemala shows increases in all forms of violence against women during Pérez Molina's corrupt regime (2012–15). Between 2009 and 2015, sexual violence rates against women doubled. While this escalation of violence against women was the continuation of violence against women that had been steadily rising since 2002, femicides (homicide rates for women) more than doubled, from 317 female homicides in 2002 to 854 in 2015.[25] Violence against Indigenous men and women in Guatemala also escalated as rural Maya sought to assert their rights to historic lands and protested against international hydroelectric projects to build dams on their lands as well as mineral exploitation.

The exemption from punishment for carrying out social cleansing is not without precedent. A Guatemalan newspaper headline in

1971 read, "Thirteen Corpses on Slopes of Pacaya Volcano: Six Iden-
tifed as Petty Criminals and Rapists, the Rest Unknown." The *New
York Times* writer Victor Perera explained that "it was said that vigi-
lante groups were 'purifying' the countryside and cleaning the courts
of their overload."[26] The general ambience of impunity surrounding
Guatemala's very high homicide rates also gives cover to contemporary clandestine groups trying to stop women's and human rights
nongovernmental organizations (NGOs) from pushing for justice. In
2001, a group of armed men entered the offices of a women's NGO in
the center of the capital and beat and raped the women there. All this
took place just one block from a police station. When I began
researching this book, Fredy Pecerrelli, president of the Guatemalan
Forensic Anthropology Foundation,[27] was denouncing death threats
to his sister. I received emails from Fredy, the Guatemalan Human
Rights Commission, and Amnesty International detailing the threats
he received. One read:

> I have been watching you like eagles [*sic*], you will die in a short
> period of time we have an order to make that damn director of the
> FAFG suffer. Everyone in your family is watched. For a long time we
> forgot about the shit of your sister. We saw her in the IGSS [public
> hospital with a morgue]. Damn her. She will suffer because of her
> brother. We will rape her and chop her into pieces. Omar Giron will
> find her and be a widower. Then, if he continues going out, we will
> capture him he will never imagine what we can do. In the FAFG they
> will be wearing black but not only for the relatives of Freddy, but
> worse for all their members of high rank. REVOLUTIONARIES OF
> SHIT. All must die in the Zone 12 in our attack. The list is long but
> your day will come FREDDY [*sic*] after we kill your entire family.[28]

This threat was directed at Fredy Pecerrelli through his sister's
body. Like the violence of the counterinsurgency of the 1980s,

women are targets in their own right but also by virtue of their relationship to male relatives. In the 1980s, the adolescent niece of a human rights activist was gang-raped by a squad of state agents who told her she was being raped because her uncle was a "subversive."[29] Repressive structures place women and their bodies on the front lines of retaliation against their male relatives in the same way that patriarchal structures place women under the "protection" and "discipline" of their male relatives. In the end, this violence against women and the murder of women today is a driver of migration, and it is tied to state inaction and impunity.

5   *Paradise for Killers*

I learned about the killing of women in Guatemala through my experience accompanying Jorge Velásquez in his search for justice in the 2005 murder of his beloved daughter, Claudina Isabel. Over the decade I accompanied Jorge, the case of Claudina Isabel passed through several different prosecutors and assistant prosecutors and traveled through four different offices until finally landing at the office of the special prosecutor for victims of murder, after much insistence by her father and the BBC special *Killer's Paradise* that highlighted Claudina Isabel's case. Given the dismal track record of the Prosecutor's Office investigating homicides, it is not surprising that there was no effort whatsoever made to carry out any investigation during the first forty-eight hours after the murder—the very hours considered by experts to be vital in a murder investigation. The Prosecutor's Office did not even interview Claudina Isabel's family members until one month after her murder and only then because they sought out the Prosecutor's Office to find out what was happening with Claudina Isabel's case. As almost anyone who has ever watched a television crime show or read a novel about a police investigation knows, interviewing the victim's family is a standard protocol of any murder investigation in order to eliminate them as the primary suspects.

The Prosecutor's Office never sought out the friends and acquaintances that were last with Claudina Isabel to get their versions of what happened the night of her murder. No search was ever conducted of the vehicles in which Claudina Isabel is known to have traveled during the last twenty-four hours of her life. The only statements taken by the Prosecutor's Office were those of individuals who voluntarily and randomly presented themselves to the Prosecutor's Office to make a declaration. These statements were taken without ever having taken testimony from Claudina Isabel's parents and without ever having developed any clear objectives for interviews in the investigation. No joint meetings have ever been held among investigators who have been involved in this case to develop strategic lines of investigation. This means that all statements have simply been recorded and taken at face value. No analysis of contradictions has ever been conducted. In fact, an investigator told me that the prosecution investigators are specifically "prohibited" from discussing cases with one another. This means that prosecution investigators can develop neither victim nor perpetrator profiles because they are not comparing crimes. In real murder investigations, especially when serial murders are involved, the only hope investigators have of capturing the perpetrator is to first develop victim profiles and then use these profiles to develop perpetrator profiles—and this is only possible through the comparison of cases.[1]

The Prosecutor's Office has made no effort to locate any potential witnesses at the crime scene where Claudina Isabel's body was found. The Prosecutor's Office has not been able to develop a list of names of the people present at the party Claudina Isabel attended in the final hours of her life. Rather than interview everyone who is known to have attended and develop a list of attendees, the prosecution's response is that there were no formal invitations and no formal list of invitees. Thus the Prosecutor's Office is unable to develop a list of those attending the party. Searches of the homes of primary suspects did not take place until three months after Claudina Isabel's murder. There has been no real search for a weapon. It was not until June 2006, ten months after her murder, that the prosecution began to interview people about Claudina Isabel's murder. Still, these interviews do not appear to have included any preparation to clarify where Claudina Isabel was and with whom during the last hours of her life. The Prosecutor's Office has not been able to collect complete telephone registers of those last seen with or last in communication with Claudina Isabel. In 2007, two years after her murder, her cell phone was still in use, though the Prosecutor's Office made no effort to determine its whereabouts. Using Claudina Isabel's account information, Ana María and Jorge were able to log in, view, and track the latest activity on her cell phone. Although it is likely that some two years after the murder, the phone had probably passed through many hands, it would still have been useful for the prosecutor to trace it and track its usage.

One of the most striking aspects of Claudina Isabel's case is that it was actually a case that was being investigated—at least according to the MP. Most cases end where Claudina Isabel's would have ended had her father not used all his resources to push for an investigation. Her case would have ended with an autopsy report that did not even include her name, despite the fact that she was identified by her mother on the same day as the autopsy. This makes suspect prosecutor and police claims of vast numbers of feminicide victims lacking identification—implying they were never identified and/or claimed by family members. We do not know how many women's victim files lack names due to the disinterest of prosecutor, police, and morgue personnel to attach a name to the victim. We do know that it is harder to understand the phenomenon of feminicide and find justice when victims are left nameless.

In his search for justice, Jorge has sought assistance and accompaniment from anyone willing to listen and help, and also from those who become more willing to do their jobs when they feel they are being monitored. Jorge is the only family member of a murder victim in the BBC documentary who was willing to grant a release for his face and name to be seen when the documentary aired in Guatemala; the other victims' family members featured by the BBC feared reprisals and did not grant releases. Jorge has met with international rights organizations and diplomatic missions. He has worked with Amnesty International to publicize Claudina Isabel's case internationally, which led to it being named an emblematic case of the Guatemalan feminicide.[2] He has traveled to the United States, Canada, and the United Kingdom to draw attention to Claudina Isabel's case and the killing of women in Guatemala.

Jorge took the media savvy he gained with the BBC to the local Guatemalan channel, Guatevisión, where he gave an in-depth interview highlighting all aspects of the case, from Claudina Isabel's murder to the government response. He talked about his daughter, her Snoopy collection and her dreams of being a criminal defense lawyer. He spoke of his faith in God and his evangelical beliefs and declared, "I forgive the person or persons who killed my daughter. But that does not mean that they do not have to pay for the crime they have committed. Claudina Isabel was assassinated at the invitation that impunity gives assassins." And a year after his daughter's death, he held the Guatemalan government responsible: "The Guatemalan State is incapable of guaranteeing the basic right to life to its citizens. Claudina Isabel died because of the indifference of the authorities."[3] The Guatevisión news director, Haroldo Sánchez, was so moved by the story that he featured Claudina Isabel again on his station—this second time as a special half-hour program with an intimate portrait of Claudina Isabel's life. Who was Claudina Isabel? What were her dreams? How is she remembered? As Jorge explained to me, "It is important for people to know who Claudina Isabel was and who she would have been. When they took her life, they also took the lives of the children she would have had and the contribution she would have made to the world. We all lost something that day."

Part of the moral of Claudina Isabel's story and perhaps what made it so powerful to the Guatevisión news director is that Claudina Isabel was a beautiful young woman who was a law student from a conservative, evangelical, upper-middle-class family. Claudina Isabel was not the prototype of the female murder victim featured in newspaper articles or dismissed by the police as nameless gang members left unclaimed by their families. Indeed, in the BBC documentary, her brother Pablo Andrés said, "My sister was a good person and they took her for a nobody. They should investigate the nobodies. No matter what they look like, the murders should be investigated. That's their job. No one is really a nobody."[4]

In his media appearances, Jorge challenges popular opinion that blames the victims for their own murders. He says, "We can be victims like anyone else. We Guatemalans think that the cadavers that appear are of people who were involved in something."[5] This idiomatic phrase, "involved in something," harkens back to the early 1980s when the tortured bodies of supposed "subversives" would appear on the streets, and in popular slang, these deaths were attributed to "andaban en algo" (they were involved in something). This *andaba en algo* from the past is now the refrain for the bodies of women that show up in the streets. Instead of asking who killed the women or any other question, the answer is simply "andaba in gangs" or "andaba as a prostitute." Friends and relatives of victims and rights advocates live with the fear of guilt by association, which is the flipside of andaba en algo. It is why some families do not claim the bodies of their murdered loved ones or pursue justice. It is how individuals can be marked by entering the Prosecutor's Office or meeting with victims' groups. I have always felt most myself when I am asked to help others to fill a gap of need. As an anthropologist, I have always loved field research because it is the place where curiosity is most rewarded. As an invited participant observer, my relationship with Jorge is reciprocal. We share our different worldviews. We challenge one another. We learn from each other, and we both learn to see and experience the world a bit differently as a result. Accompanying Jorge, I must have suspended my judgment about the risks of the work we were doing because it never occurred to me that I "was involved in something" as I traveled around Guatemala City with Jorge to meet with prosecutors, police, human rights advocates, and ambassadors. When I accepted the files of other high-impact human rights cases to send to my colleagues for forensic review, I knew the materials were sensitive, so I only sent them to the United States with trusted friends who would hand carry the files. They were called high-impact because they were complex, premeditated crimes that implicated very powerful Guatemalans. As I think back about those grisly cases, I mostly remember sharing a belief that with sufficient evidence, justice might be possible.

"We've Come for the Garbage"

He came at six in the morning while my husband was in the shower.[6] He rang the doorbell. Because I was leaving on a morning flight to Tokyo, I was up and dressed. I dashed through our front garden to the metal door and opened the little window to see who was ringing the bell so early because I did not want the doorbell to ring again and awaken my baby. Through the window grate, I saw a man standing firmly, almost bored as he waited. Tall for a Guatemalan, he was about my height and had shortly cropped, dark hair. Erect in stature, he appeared trim in a navy Adidas running suit. His bearing belied his civilian clothing. I immediately knew he was from the army. "What do you want?," I asked him. He tilted his head back in an arrogant stance, and looking directly in my eyes, he said, "We've come for the garbage."

I knew he had not come for the garbage. Garbage in Guatemala is picked up by poor boys in dirty, smelly clothes. Boys who look as if they have not bathed in weeks, which may be the case, or it may simply be the filth they acquire by spending the day being transported around the city in the garbage truck because they actually sit in the garbage and sift through it as they go from stop to stop. I knew our garbage boys well. I always gave them some food and a tip. Sometimes I gave them clothes. I also packed anything sharp or broken in a separate bag and told the garbage boy about it in an effort to prevent injury. The garbage boys were often barefoot, and their hair looked sooty and stuck out in different directions as if they had just awoken. This healthy man at my door was no garbage boy.

"At this hour?," I asked. Shaking my head and swallowing my fear, I answered my own question, "No, there is no garbage here." And the trim man in the Adidas suit held up his cell phone in my direction as he said, "We'll be back. There is garbage here, and we always get the garbage." I said nothing as I closed the window. Later I realized he had taken my photo with his cell phone.

This is how the threats began. I still flew to Tokyo that morning, mostly because I had fronted the cost of the plane ticket to give a keynote lecture at United Nations University about the Guatemalan peace process and I could not afford to not be reimbursed for the $2,300. I wept most of the way to Tokyo. I was worried sick about my two-year-old daughter. And they, whoever they are, already know that. The people who make threats already know what matters most to you. And if you are a mother or a father, they know it is your children.

The only thing truly surprising about this early morning threat that was almost elegant in its brutal understatement is that it happened in March 2007 and not earlier. It is not that my years of work in Guatemala had been without threats; it is that previous threats were more general, not directed specifically at me and my family.

More than a decade earlier, when I was working with the Guatemalan Forensic Anthropology Foundation in the summer of 1994 (two years before the peace accords were signed) on the exhumation of the clandestine cemetery of army massacre victims in Plan de Sánchez, high in the mountains above the municipality of Rabinal, the FAFG received what we called the postmodern threat: a fax. It read, "Deja los muertos en pas [sic] hijos de puta" (Leave the dead in peace [peace was misspelled] sons of whores). The same day we received the threat, the local and national office of the Human Rights Ombudsman received the same faxed threat. Meanwhile, local Achi Maya peasants received the kinds of threats they had grown accustomed to: they were called to the local army base in Rabinal, where the army commander told them, "Those anthropologists, journalists, and internationals are all guerrilla. You know what happens when you support the guerrilla. Leave the dead in peace, or the violence of the past will return." The difference between being a Maya peasant and a member of the forensic team is that we forensic anthropologists were all pretty sure that the army would not kill all of us and somehow found safety in this analysis. The Maya peasants had no such luxury when carrying out their complicated political calculus about whether to move forward with the exhumation. After all, the graves were the evidence that the army had no compunction about slaughtering 268 Maya peasants, mostly women and children. Still as the forensic team and the massacre survivors shared news of receiving threats, we all agreed to move forward with the exhumation because stopping it would leave the community with even less political space than they had had when we began our work. So we called in national and international press and human rights NGOs to bring attention to our work and the struggle of the massacre survivors.[7]

That same summer, I interviewed a high-ranking member of the Guatemalan government who was involved in the peace negotiations. The interview was at the National Palace. He was a civilian. I taped the interview. I was surprised by how much he knew about the day-to-day workings of the team in Rabinal and Plan de Sánchez. Clearly someone was giving the government information about our movement and even our conversations. Without naming anyone, he directed my attention to Tom,[8] an international member of the team who had made some disparaging if warranted comments about the Guatemalan army. Then the civilian functionary said, "No one should believe that a US passport protects him from the army. If the army is insulted, it will strike back."

In Guatemalan parlance, this was not a threat but a warning, which gives one the possibility of stepping back in line, whereas a threat does not. And I thought, "I cannot believe that I am in the National Palace and that a member of the peace negotiating team is menacing a US citizen member of the forensic team and telling me the army will strike any one of us if they don't like what we say." And I noticed the hanging lights were vibrating and emitting a kind of hum as the lights dimmed and brightened. As soon as I left the palace, I went straight back to my hotel to listen to the tape. I was so excited to have proof of the menacing collusion between the civilian government and the army that sought to halt the exhumations. The beginning of the taped interview is perfectly clear, as is the end. But in the middle, just when the civilian functionary gave me the warning, the voices are garbled behind that hum from the lights, except on my tape, the hum is louder than the voices, which seem to be pulled into slow motion, sounding like talking under water.

If you look at your recording equipment, you will notice there is a tag that says something about compliance with the Federal Communications Commission: *This device complies with Part 15 of the FCC Rules. Operation is subject to the following two conditions: (1). This device may not cause harmful interference; and, (2). This device must accept any interference received, including interference that may cause undesired operation.* Apparently, my device had accepted interference from the office of army intelligence of the Estado Mayor (the high command of the army), which had its offices right above the civilian functionary in 1994.

Four years earlier, in a 1990 Secret Memo on Guatemalan intelligence capabilities, US Defense Intelligence Agency agents in Guatemala describe the top floor of the National Palace (the presidential palace) as occupied by the Guatemalan Ministry of Defense Intelligence (D-2), including director and subdirector offices, a reception area, "interrogation cubicles," a small auditorium, and an intelligence center that has maps of Nicaragua, El Salvador, and Cuba.[9] The memo also provides DIA headquarters in Washington, DC, and other US intelligence agencies with an overview of Guatemalan intelligence gathering by interception of signals, referred to as "sigint." US DIA describes the Guatemalan D-2 as a "human intelligence organization." The agency also reports that "D-2 officers have admitted conducting technical surveillance (wire taps) and surveillance on US citizens [no other information provided]."[10] It is not clear from the memo if the note about no further information meant that the US DIA had no further information on the intelligence gathered or the gathering methods. In either case, there is no suggestion in the memo that the agency questioned D-2 methods, targets, or intelligence gathered.

While D-2 is the official name of the army's intelligence structure, many Guatemalans still refer to it as G-2, as it was called in the 1980s. In July 1994, the Immigration and Refugee Board of Canada reported contentious relations between the Estado Mayor Presidencial (EMP) and the G-2 because of "overlapping functions and questions of hierarchy."[11] Shortly after Ramiro de León assumed the presidency in 1993, he appointed Colonel Otto Pérez Molina (who had previously headed the G-2 and would later be elected president, only to fall from grace in an epic scandal) as the new director of the EMP, which would indicate either a consolidation of intelligence agencies or a power coup of one over the other.

Whether EMP, G-2, or D-2, many Guatemalans will tell you that army intelligence had its offices in the National Palace in order to monitor the words and actions of the president and vice president and their civilian staff. Despite the transformation or renaming of G-2 to D-2 and the apparent 2003 transmorphing of the EMP into the Secretaría de Asuntos Administrativos y de Seguridad de la Presidencia (SAAS; Secretariat of Administrative Affairs and Presidential Security), these intelligence practices of the past continued through the 1996 signing of the Peace Accords and also past the Peace Accord deadline of 1999 for the dissolution of the EMP.[12]

In September 2008, President Alvaro Colom announced the resignation of his director of presidential security, Carlos Quintanilla, and denounced wiretapping in the National Palace and his home. In a classified memo, then–US ambassador Stephen G. McFarland summarized a meeting with Colom about the wiretapping and concluded that the president did not know who was working with him or against him. Colom did not know if Quintanilla had done the wiretapping, only that he should have kept the president's quarters swept clean of such devices. McFarland was also unable to clarify the command responsibility for the wiretapping.[13] Was it Quintanilla? Did he do it for someone else? Who gave the order? The army? The police? The oligarchy?

My own experience and the wiretapping of President Colom leads me to wonder exactly how many people are involved in army and police surveillance. The 1990 declassified US DIA Secret Memo also provides a list of names of forty-eight known intelligence officers and reports fifteen hundred paid informants.[14] It also lists 1st Lieutenant Luis Ronaldo Cámbara Deras, assistant to the Conference of American Armies Liaison, as having a "special intelligence collection assignment against non-governmental organizations working in Guatemala."[15] In 1994, the Immigration and Refugee Board of Canada reported the 1993 defection of a G-2 agent who denounced G-2 "planning and executing kidnappings, torture and murder."[16] While many people had previously made these same allegations, the agent shed new light on two critical issues that have fed corruption and impunity in Guatemala. First, he outlined the deep links and transactional relationship between intelligence agents and civilians who serve as informers in exchange for money or power. Second, he explained that though the victim's alleged participation or support of the guerrillas was always the pretext for torture and murder, "the majority of the killings were really over personal disputes unrelated to the guerrillas"[17]—meaning that the majority of the killings were driven by corruption, power struggles, and petty rivalries.

How does this intelligence and surveillance work? Who decides when to follow? When to frighten? When to sequester? When to harm? How does a gringa like me play into all of this? What are the stakes? What tips the balance? Exactly how does all this violence work?

In 1997, when I was living in Guatemala for a year doing research for my dissertation, I was followed by an unmarked army vehicle when I was driving with Asha, my German shepherd, back to Guatemala City from an exhumation of Maya genocide victims in San Martín, Jilotepeque, Chimaltenango. There were two men in a gray pickup with darkly polarized windows and an antenna on the roof. They tailed me. At first, I thought they wanted to pass me, so I slowed down. This only brought them closer to my bumper. I increased my speed so much that I had to pass several vehicles in front of me, and somewhat dangerously. They did the same on the winding, two-lane mountain road. And they made a point of letting me know they were behind me by almost hitting the back of my Isuzu Trooper. I sped up again, and they sped up again. I slowed down, and they slowed down.

This cat-and-mouse game went on for more than an hour. I was terrorized. I realized they were definitely following me and meant to frighten or injure me.

As I got closer to Guatemala City, I started thinking about where I should go. "Can't go to the police station, they are not going to help. Can't go to the US Embassy because it is so far behind barricades, and reaching the periphery of the embassy would only put me into contact with local Guatemala police, again no help from them. Can't go home. On the off chance that they don't know where I live, I am certainly not going to lead them to my house. Can't go to a hotel or shopping center because I would first have to enter a large underground parking lot—the stuff of stalking nightmares." I considered driving to the forensic team's office but worried that I might find myself alone with one police guard. What can a gringa in distress do? Where should she go?

Then I thought of my mechanic and his brother who were both burly ladinos and had a large repair garage with very large and heavy metal doors to protect their expensive equipment. I drove directly to them. I pulled in my car and told them about the truck of men following me. They immediately pulled me behind them and gathered together, making themselves visible to the road outside, with menacing looks and heavy wrenches in hand as they closed the garage door. At their suggestion, I stayed inside the garage with them for an hour or so. They gave me coffee and sweet breads. Then they drove me home. One of them drove my car back to my house in one direction, and the other drove me to the house using a different route. I don't know if the men who followed me saw me again, but I never saw them.

I was undeterred. It is hard to explain why. Though I often tried to explain to my mother and finally reached a form of détente with her on the topic. What could I say to her when, like the civilian functionary, she reminded me that my US passport was not a bullet-proof shield and that it did not stop bombs from falling from the sky or grenades from flying through windows. I never felt immortal, exactly, I just seldom felt afraid, and when I did, it was temporary. Moments of fear were like war correspondent stories to be shared with others who did the same kind of work and were told as a kind of cathartic joke over a beer. The last laugh being on the mystery men who made the threats, because, after all, we were sitting together telling stories of how we gamed them and were still digging up graves or doing other human rights work.

But somehow the equation is different when the threat is singularly directed at you and your family. People who are threatened become isolated and at the same time further isolate themselves for fear of putting themselves or their family members at greater risk, or passing their precarious condition on to friends through Guatemala's ideology of guilt by association. Ultimately, people who receive threats become their own jailers.

After the garbage incident, we stopped going out as a family because I was afraid we would be run off the road and die in a "car accident." We did not go out to dinner with friends or away to Lake Atitlán for weekends, even though we were repeatedly invited. I could not visit my Maya friends in the highlands because the trip was too dangerous and I feared placing them in danger with my presence.

We never left our daughter without at least one parent, and we always had at least one other international staying in our home. Without making a conscious decision, I stopped leaving the house. I only left with Jorge to go to the Office of the Human Rights Ombudsman or the Prosecutor's Office to push for investigation of his daughter's murder. I was too fearful to take a taxi because it could be carjacked, or might not be a real taxi, or might even be a taxi that worked for whoever was threatening me. I did not want my husband's employees to take me to any high-impact human rights case meetings or to drop off any envelopes because I did not want them to be marked for surveillance or worse. And my husband could not take me because we could not leave our daughter, and I was terrified by the idea of us all being in one car together. I could not drive the car because I was afraid to go by myself, afraid I would be disappeared. I did not want to leave a car unattended because I was afraid of having drugs planted in it (as had happened to a friend of mine in the past). I could not talk on the phone about the threats because the assumption is that whoever is making the threats is listening to my phone calls. One of my research assistants received threats; they were written all over the wall at the university: "We will rape you to death." Was this related to work she was doing for me? She told me they were unrelated, and I chose to believe her because violence was so pervasive and I felt powerless.

Little by little, threats filled up every corner of my life. One afternoon, our daughter was playing in the little walled garden patio in front of our house. The walls must have been about eight feet high. She was 2 ½ years old. She came up to me in the living room and said, "Mommy, there is a person in the garden. Can I touch it?" Her nanny and I looked at each other in terror. At my instruction, Marlena grabbed my daughter and took her into our bedroom and locked the door.[18] I called her father in his office a few blocks away as I closed and locked all the doors. Raúl came running home with the messenger and graphic designer from his press, with the women from the office trailing close behind. They burst into the empty garden and then into the house. The garden was small; no one could hide anywhere.

By this time, Marlena was playing with my daughter. I gently asked her to show me where she had seen the person in the garden. She took me to the large pepper tree in the center of the patio. She pointed to the ground on the back side of the tree. "There Mommy. See, there is the person," she said. I looked down and started to laugh. She had been asking me if she could touch a little doll in the dirt. I picked it up and washed it for her. It was a three-inch Lara Croft Tomb Raider doll.

Over the next few months, the fears awakened by that little doll would find new places to dwell on a near-daily basis. A neighbor informed us that a man with a gruff voice called looking for me. The call had gone to her home because she lived in the house connected to ours. Apparently, she had the original phone that had belonged to the home before it had been divided for renting. She said, "They called for Victoria Sanford. I said, 'You are mistaken, there is no one here by that name.'" She explained that we should know about the call, because the caller was angry and said, "It doesn't matter, we will find her." She was concerned. "It reminds me of *before*," she said. "I thought you should know."

Surveillance seemed to increase by the day. Whenever we left the house, there was a young ladina woman sitting on the curb reporting on passersby. "They are leaving now," she would say. When Jorge and I arrived at the office of a human rights group to talk about his daughter's case and some other cases, we were watched by a man in an unmarked pickup without license plates. He glared at us as we walked past him and on up to the door of the office. My neck stiffened. I felt his eyes piercing the back of my head. I thought he was going to shoot us. When we got to the front step of the human rights office, there were three police officers milling around almost blocking our access to the door in an aggressive, accusatory kind of way.

A woman called my nanny and told her a lot of personal information about her and her family—a way to scare my nanny and let us know that they knew who cared for our daughter. Then our landlords came to our home—the little half house that we had leased for a year—asking for it to be returned immediately. The señora wrung her hands and reiterated, "I know you are honorable people, but you must go." Sometimes surveillance is an effective form of intimidation.

But Jorge was not intimidated. He drove me to see the human rights lawyers so that I could tell them exactly what had happened. We decided that I should notify the US Embassy. I wanted them to know that if I died in an accident, it would need to be investigated. Just as I had accompanied Jorge, he accompanied me to the US Embassy so I could report the surveillance and intimidation. When I met with the chief political officer, I wondered if he would take seriously this odd collection of threats and experiences. I was mistaken. Guatemala had made him war-weary in less than two years. He told me he had previously been posted in Argentina for two rotations and had been involved with investigations of rights violations there. He said, "I thought I knew everything about political violence after serving in Argentina. But in eighteen months in Guatemala, I have learned a whole new vocabulary for killing. I never knew there were so many words for murder." Then he asked me, "When are you leaving?"

Two weeks later, I was in Costa Rica with my daughter and her nanny. We stayed there for a month. I couldn't return to my apartment in New York City because it was sublet and my nanny did not have a visa to enter the United States. So we decided to stay in San José with our eldest daughter, Gabriela. Still on summer break, I used the opportunity to write *Guatemala: Del genocidio al feminicidio*. Thus I redefined my ongoing work on Claudina Isabel's case and found a way to continue to support the brave efforts of Jorge and the human rights lawyers working on his and other high-impact human rights cases. And just as his case did not end with the publication of *Guatemala: Del genocidio al feminicidio*,[19] the other cases continued as well.

6 Marked Women

The Dangers of Saying No to the Gang

Women who live in gang-controlled areas face particularly serious threats to their lives and freedom. The acceptance of violence against women combines with the gang's insistence on control over the population within their territory, and the result is extreme violence, especially sexual violence. Even minor interactions with gangs can be incredibly dangerous, because they have the dual significance of acquiescence to the specific demand and acceptance of the gang's control and power. However, when the demand is for a sexual relationship with a woman, then there is a treble significance: acquiescence to the relationship, acceptance of the gang's power, and acknowledgment of the gang member's position of dominance as a male. Thus a young woman who refuses a gang member's proposition is threatening not only his power as a gang member, but his status as a male within the social hierarchy. Indeed, women who are "gang members" are likely to be, themselves, nonconsensually involved with male gang members owing to patriarchal societal norms as well as gang structures. So women who become "disposable" because of their gang associations were likely never interested in gang membership to begin with; rather they were coerced.

Therefore, young women who are sexual targets of gang members are in great danger. They cannot exercise their basic rights to life and freedom of movement, much less their right to control their own sexual relationships. If they refuse to accept the gang member's advances, then the gang will retaliate against them for standing up to their authority, often with gang rape or murder. But even if a young woman or girl does accept the gang member's romantic or sexual advances, she is still in danger, because she has no control within the relationship. If the gang member gets angry, or tired of her, then she is once again at risk of being raped or murdered. And once a girl or young woman has a relationship with a gang member, she is associated with that gang and therefore also at risk of being caught up in the gang's actions and harmed by other violent groups.

This girl or young woman is also perceived within her community as a gang member, as gang member property, or as marked by gang members by virtue of the relationship, whether real or perceived, with a gang member. This association or perceived association makes the girl or young woman a threat to her family and her neighborhood, which will isolate, hide from, or avoid her. Thus she has no safe haven to run to for sanctuary if she seeks to flee the gang member.

The dangers facing girls and young women in this type of situation are well understood, and recognized, within Guatemalan society. Once a girl or young woman refuses to submit to a gang's sexual control, she often becomes a pariah within her social network, because her family and friends know that their association with her puts them at risk with the gang. If she stays in her home, then the gang may attack her family in retaliation for her insubordination.

A friend of mine lives in a gang-controlled area. He works hard and has always refused to become involved in crime or gangs, and for the most part they have respected his decision because he has known them for a long time and they trust he is not an *oreja* (ear, meaning "spy"). But he has three younger sisters, and he is absolutely terrified for them. He says, "As they get older, and become prettier, they are in more and more danger." When his sisters come to stay with him, he does not allow them out of the house. He doesn't want people in the neighborhood to even lay eyes on them. Because if a gang member decides that he wants one of the sisters, then the whole family will be in an impossible situation. If she says no, then the gang will retaliate. The gang will not only hurt her; they will hurt her family and her friends. So he keeps them inside, and they all live in fear.

When it comes to gangs, women have few options. A young woman who refuses to respond to a gang member's advances is very brave. She is not only refusing him; she is refusing to accept the rules that her society has placed on her. Unfortunately, that decision also places her in terrible danger.

Manuela's Refusal

Manuela does not remember when her parents divorced.[1] She does remember moving from living with her mother to her elderly aunt's after her stepfather tried to rape her when she was 6 years old. After that, she lived alone with her aunt in a poor barrio in Guatemala City. Though they were poor, she went to school. Her mother sent the aunt money to buy her school supplies and meet her most basic needs. When she started high school, she could walk or take the bus—it was a ten block trip from her aunt's house.

Manuela grew up watching the local gang control her neighborhood through violence and extortion. Armed gang members were on every block. The gang collected weekly tributes or taxes from all houses, including from Manuela's elderly aunt. She always paid because she knew the gang would kill her or Manuela if she did not.

They had witnessed gang killings in their neighborhood. Impunity was such that the gang carried out its violence against those who did not pay tribute in a public spectacle for the entire neighborhood to witness. In this way, the gang reminded all the neighbors of the cost of refusing to pay. By the time Manuela started high school, some girls and boys there were gang members. This terrified her and her aunt. High schools, like the streets of Guatemala, are a prime recruiting location for new gang members. Manuela decided to do everything possible to avoid the gang members at school.

Two years into high school, Manuela thought she had escaped the gang, until the local gang leader, Rafael, decided that she should be his girlfriend. Rafael was in his early twenties and well known in the neighborhood for murder and extortion. Even before he introduced himself to 15-year-old Manuela, she knew who he was because everyone feared him. At first Rafael told her that he wanted to take her to nice places and buy her nice things. He would show her the wad of cash he carried in his pocket. He told her she was pretty and he would protect her. Though she was scared, his flirting seemed harmless because he was not using any violence. She even felt flattered because he was flirting with her in such a sweet way. Initially, she thought she could hold him at bay much in the same way she avoided the gang members at school.

Soon, when she walked to school, those gang members on street corners would say, "Look how cute Rafael's girlfriend is." That really scared her. She thought it might all blow over if she stayed home from school for a few days, but that just made Rafael come to her house. He did not come alone. He came with several armed gang members and told her that he wanted her to be his girlfriend and join his gang. Manuela did not know what to do. She told him that she had never had a boyfriend and would have to think about it. He gave her one day. "I will be back for you tomorrow," he said as he left.

When he returned alone the following day, Manuela thought he might accept her refusal. When she politely declined, explaining that she wanted to focus on schoolwork and was not ready for a relationship, he slapped her, punched her, kicked her, and told her that she had one more day to decide. "I am giving you another day to recognize that you belong to me. I will be back tomorrow and you will accept," he said. "If you refuse me, you will have the same fate as all whores. I will give you to my gang after I am done with you." Manuela fled Guatemala in fear for her life that same day.

A Meeting with the Dark Side

In 2007, after an international scandal involving elite Guatemalan police in the massacre of Salvadoran representatives to the Central American Parliament (PARLACEN), Adela Torrebiarte was named to replace the implicated Carlos Vielman as minister of the interior.[2] A member of one of Guatemala's elite families, Torrebiarte distinguished herself in the early 1990s as the founder of Madres Angustiadas (Anguished Mothers), which was a group of mostly elite women seeking recognition of their suffering because of kidnappings for extortion and serving as an oligarchic alternative to the organizations of the families of the disappeared such as the Mutual Support Group (GAM), Families of the Disappeared of Guatemala (FAMDEGUA), and the Coordinating Committee of Widows of Guatemala (CONAVIGUA). Torrebiarte's son was kidnapped in 1995. Many Guatemalans told me that Torrebiarte had invited Víctor Rivera to Guatemala in the mid-1990s to help her resolve this kidnapping and that he seemed to serve as a henchman on call for the oligarchy. Rivera was a shadowy figure working with the Salvadoran regime before the peace accords. Many believed he was a CIA operative. He arrived in Guatemala ready to use his skills and training to help resolve kidnappings. It appears his record was pretty strong in terms of finding the victim, who sometimes survived the attack by Rivera's anti-kidnapping squad. Though Rivera never had an official position within the Ministry of the Interior, a few months after the

PARLACEN killings, Jorge Velásquez was summoned to a meeting with Rivera to discuss the status of his daughter's case.

Jorge came over to my house to tell me about the invitation to speak with Rivera about Claudina Isabel's murder investigation. We made a list of the different possible motivations. My first thought was that when Torrebiarte entered her new office as minister of the interior, she must have found 15,000 to 20,000 letters and postcards requesting investigation into Claudina Isabel's murder. Her case had become the paradigmatic case of feminicide in Amnesty International's worldwide campaign to raise awareness about the killing of women in Guatemala.[3] As a result, Jorge had received more than 11,000 postcards and letters of support from around the world. He had organized them by country, shape, and size. They came from all over the world: South Korea, India, Ireland, Mexico, the United States, and countries in Europe, Africa, and the Middle East. Some were group letters from churches or class projects with beautiful drawings. Many were just kind words of sympathy and solidarity from anonymous citizens of faraway countries. I was moved to imagine a group of South Korean churchgoers gathering to make a beautiful card and send their support to the father of a feminicide victim in Guatemala. Then I said to Jorge, "Torrebiarte must have 40,000 letters and postcards because most people write to the government and skip the individual contact. At least that is what I do. A lot more people will write to the government seeking justice. I am guessing at least four to one."

So I was sure that tens of thousands of letters and cards must have gone to the Ministry of the Interior. And I remembered my friend and colleague Roberto Lemus telling me that when he became the justice of the peace in a town in Quiché, he found his office full of boxes of letters and cards from an Amnesty campaign seeking investigation into army massacres; even his desk drawers were full of the cards and letters. I imagined all these unopened cards and letters were there waiting for Torrebiarte. I hoped that Torrebiarte had the courage to do what Judge Lemus had done: write to everyone with a return address and seek assistance in the investigation. In Judge Lemus's case, this led to the first exhumation of a clandestine grave in San José Pacho de Lemoa in 1992, led by Dr. Clyde Snow with support from the American Association for the Advancement of Science (AAAS) and the Argentine Forensic Anthropology Team.[4] Though Judge Lemus was forced into exile shortly thereafter, his courage and this initial work led to the founding of the Guatemalan Forensic Anthropology Foundation that continues to exhume clandestine graves.

Whether out of genuine interest in the case or seeing this as a way to win public confidence in Torrebiarte's capacity, Rivera told Jorge that the new minister wanted to get Claudina Isabel's case moving. It is also possible that Rivera knew that we had spent a lot of time with Human Rights Ombudsman staff working on Claudina Isabel's case and consulting with international experts. Maybe he knew I had become involved in other high-impact cases as a result of these consultations. Or maybe this was a way for him to get to Álvaro Matus, the prosecutor, who was assigned to PARLACEN as well as Claudina Isabel's investigation.

Rivera had a large office with his own conference room adjacent to the office of then–vice-minister of the interior, Vinicio Gómez. When we arrived, the interactions between Rivera and Gómez were such that I initially believed Gómez was Rivera's secretary, not the vice-minister of the interior. Some even suggest that Rivera chose Torrebiarte to replace Vielman. We were well aware of Rivera's reputation. We knew that the Ministry of the Interior was a hornet's nest, but we thought that perhaps Rivera might be able to get the case moving. So we took a deep breath and decided to go to the meeting.

At that April meeting to discuss Claudina Isabel's case, Matus was oddly friendly toward me, though obviously nervous. It was unclear to me whether Matus's newfound friendliness and nervousness derived from his fear of Rivera, or because he had no answers to provide to Rivera's very basic questions about the prosecutor's investigation into Claudina Isabel's murder, or if it was related to their joint responsibilities to investigate the PARLACEN case as well as the notorious Pavón prison massacre.

Rivera sat at the head of a long table in a short-sleeved, checkered cotton shirt, casual Friday style. He had the bearing of an active military man who does calisthenics early every morning. Unlike Matus, who had dark circles under his eyes and looked like a hungover mobster in his padded-shoulder suit, Rivera bounced with energy. He said, "We are going to be pro-positive! We are going to resolve this case." He had a white binder with INTERPOL biographies. As he began to talk with us, he was also looking at a biography of Jorge. When Jorge noticed this, he requested a copy. "I would like to know what information you have about me," he said. Rivera opened the binder and gave the pages to Jorge. They were general biographical bits of information: birthdate, marital status, employment, bank account and property information. It was disquieting, but Rivera seemed unperturbed by the information as well as Jorge's request.

Rivera began to question Matus about the case. Matus was mostly unable to answer any of Rivera's questions. Jorge's lawyer, Carlos Pop, provided a thorough legal analysis of the case and its status. Jorge shared his frustration with the lack of movement on the case. It was unclear whether Matus was listening to their interventions. Rivera concluded the meeting with a list of standard investigative protocols for Matus and his staff to follow. Jorge agreed to provide a copy of the case with the information he had collected with Carlos, the PDH, and me. We left the meeting feeling that maybe there might be movement in the case, but we also felt apprehensive, lacking trust in both Rivera and Matus.

This Is How Impunity Works

This is how it works.[5] Everyone has the recourse of violence. But some people, because they are very rich or powerful or because they are important to people who are very rich or powerful, have more recourse to more violence. And because violence has magical qualities, this violence is structured in such a way that these same people can claim innocence or ignorance of its deployment even as terror imbues each moment of everyday life.

This is how it works. It started with the divorce. The man was mean and abusive. The woman was desperate for safety. She fled the marriage with their baby son. She filed for divorce. She won a divorce judgment. He refused to pay child support. Bravely, or innocently, she took him to court to demand that he support his son. The man told the judge, I will give her diapers or formula, but I won't give her money because she has a lover.

Taken aback, the judge, who was decidedly modern for Guatemala, said that the court ordered the man to provide a monthly monetary maintenance to the mother of his child. It was her choice how to spend it, not his. As for the lover, that was not the concern of the court, and neither should it be the concern of the man.

This man was an itinerant vendor of chewing gum, candies, and cigarettes. He would tell you that he was in the import-export business. He would take the bus from Guatemala City up to the Mexican border, a four-hour ride. He would walk across the border to buy Mexican gum, candies, and cigarettes that he would sell in Guatemala City to small tiendas—the little neighborhood storefronts tended by the señora of the house. Over the years, he came to know most of the immigration and customs officials on either side of the border. This made him useful to people with other kinds of import-export interests. Soon he had enough money to buy a truck. He no longer took the bus. He felt powerful. He was furious when he left the court. He was angry with the woman and the system. He had no plans to pay a monthly maintenance. He was going to punish the woman for having a lover.

This is how it works. His friends at the border have friends in police units in Guatemala City. He decides to make use of his recourse to violence.

One day, the mother of his son is driving with her mother. She notices two motorcycle police following close behind her. They signal to her to pull over. They swagger up to the driver's window. She says, "What did I do, officers? I haven't broken any law." They order the woman and her mother out of the vehicle. They search the car. They produce a bag full of rolls of $20 bills and a bag of white powder from a backseat that had been empty when they pulled her over. The police arrest her for drug trafficking.

This is how it works. From the jail, she calls her boss. She is secretary to the president of a large company. He sends over a lawyer who tells her not to worry. The lawyer needs someone to run an errand. He asks her, "Do you have a trustworthy friend? ¿Una persona de confianza?"

This is how it works. She calls a friend. She asks him to bring some food and magazines to her in the jail. "Can you do me a favor?," she asks. He agrees. He goes to the company offices and is given a heavy backpack by an anonymous worker. He can feel the contours of the cash contained within; he imagines thousands of bills. He is too frightened to open the backpack and look at the contents. As long as it remains closed, he does not know what is inside. He remains ignorant, innocent even. His hands shake as he delivers the bulging backpack to the judge who is waiting for him at the front door of his home.

The next day in court, she faints. A private doctor sent by the company president determines that she cannot remain in preventive detention (there is no bail available for drug trafficking charges). She is too ill for jail. She needs an IV. This means that she needs to be in a hospital. So the company president arranges for her to go to a private hospital while she awaits her trial. In order to avoid preventive detention in jail, she must spend twenty-four hours a day with an IV in her arm in a private hospital—a get-out-of-jail option available only to the wealthy and/or well connected.

Her lawyer explains to her that the judge cannot vacate the charges because she was found in possession of cocaine as well as the several thousand dollars. However, if she will plead guilty to possession for personal use, the judge can release her without charging her because she has never before been arrested. "But I don't use drugs," she says. "And I will lose custody of my son if I admit to using drugs." The lawyer reassures her that this is the best exit from an impossible situation and that she will not lose her son. He reminds her that she would spend twelve to twenty years in prison and be fined 50,000 to 1 million quetzales if she is convicted of trafficking. "These lesser charges are in your best interest and also in the interest of your son," says the lawyer.

In court, the judge accepts her guilty plea of possession of cocaine for personal use and voids the charges against her because she is a first-time offender. She leaves the court worried about what the father of her son will do next. The company president shares her concern. He talks to Víctor Rivera, who talks to the local police station commander. Rivera assigns the commander to personally supervise security at her home. The commander does not assign the two motorcycle cops from his station who planted the drugs on her. The commander periodically stands guard himself. Víctor Rivera is powerful.[6]

This is how it works. Company president outwits itinerant chewing gum importer who dabbles in petty drug trafficking. The man is enraged. He will have to take care of this himself. He continues to watch the mother of his son. The police guard has made it more difficult at her home. But they don't follow her when she goes out. He does.

He follows her to meet her lover. He follows them to a restaurant. He follows them as they stroll down the street arm in arm after lunch. They are too caught up in each other's words to notice him driving slowly behind them. When his truck is parallel to them, he lifts a machine gun to the open passenger window and fires. His son's mother shrieks in horror. He drives away.

This is how it works. She has no physical injuries but is covered with her lover's blood. Cut in half by the gunfire, he bleeds profusely. He is unable to move. Weeks later, her 34-year-old lover will die from the machine-gun strafing that severed his spinal cord, leaving him quadriplegic until his heart stopped beating following a fourth heart attack.

The day of the attack, she contemplates fleeing the country with her son. She is terrified. The next morning, there are a few lines buried in the newspaper: An itinerant chewing gum salesman was found dead in his truck on the outskirts of Guatemala City. He suffered a single bullet wound to the head. The police suspect robbery.

This is how it works. No company president is going to risk being the next victim of the enraged ex-husband of his secretary.

This is how it works. Company president outflanks itinerant chewing gum importer who dabbles in petty drug trafficking.

Jorge Struggles for Justice

At different points in Jorge's investigation into Claudina Isabel's murder, it seemed that we had narrowed down the suspects to two or three young men. On several occasions, friends and acquaintances of Jorge offered to "help him out." They would say, "None of them can be good. I can find someone to 'take care of it.'" But Jorge wanted justice, not more lawlessness. Justice works differently than violence. Jorge had lost his daughter to violence and was determined that her life would not be lost in vain. He was determined that he would stop the ongoing killing of women in Guatemala. He appealed to anyone who would listen. With his lawyer, Carlos Pop, he filed a petition with the Inter-American Commission for Human Rights against the government of Guatemala for failing to ensure Claudina Isabel's basic rights to safety, security, and a life free of discrimination. While Jorge waited, he continued to go to the Prosecutor's Office, to the police investigator's office, and to the Office of the Human Rights Ombudsman, as well as any embassy or NGO that would receive him. Often elusive, justice seems always to be slow.

7 *Bittersweet Justice*

Courts of Last Resort

A court of last resort is the highest court to which one can appeal for justice. In the Americas, the highest court beyond national courts for human rights cases is the Inter-American Court of Human Rights (IAC) in Costa Rica. Established by the Organization of American States, any member state can take a complaint directly to the Court. Individual citizens must first present their case to the Inter-American Commission for review, and they can only do this after they have exhausted avenues for legal remedies within their national system—which means they first must attempt to seek justice in their home country before they can ask the Commission to consider their case. In Guatemala in the 1980s, 1990s, and 2000s, this has meant seeking legal remedy in a national court system that is largely stacked against victims and most often corrupt. Nonetheless, victims must demonstrate an effort to resolve their case in national courts before taking their case to the Inter-American Commission.

Once the Commission has a case and decides it has merit worthy of intervention, it may attempt to resolve the case by making recommendations directly to the responsible state. If the state fails to comply or if the Commission finds the case has special merits, it can forward the case to the IAC for adjudication. The Court will make two rulings: one on the merits of the case and another on reparations. This is not a speedy process. It generally takes a decade for a successful case to travel from filing with the Commission to the Court's decision. For example, the Court ruled against the Guatemalan state in favor of the survivors of Plan de Sánchez in 2004—ten years after the exhumation of the clandestine cemetery and twenty-two years after the massacre.[1] Moreover, the IAC is not a criminal court and cannot issue jail sentences. Rather it makes moral pronouncements of state responsibility on the merits of the case and nonbinding recommendations for reparations, which means that responsibility to fulfill the Court's recommendations falls on a state government's commitment to rule of law or concern about international reputation. Generally, monetary reparations move more quickly than fulfillment of recommendations for reform or resolution of operational rule of law issues.

Though the Inter-American Court is technically the court of last resort for the Americas, recent international human rights cases have demonstrated creative ways for survivors and their advocates to pursue justice in national and international courts. Survivors have sought justice in local Guatemalan courts, immigration courts in the United States, civil courts in the United States, criminal cases in European courts, and, in the international genocide case against high-ranking Guatemalan generals led by Judge Santiago Pedraz, in the Spanish National Court. Recent Guatemalan cases demonstrate the power and usefulness of simultaneously moving forward with cases on as many fronts as possible.[2]

But back in the early 2000s, it was under the corrupt police system dominated by Vielman, Rivera, Matus, and other thugs that regular Guatemalans tried to make their daily lives while Jorge Velásquez and other victims and their families sought justice. As I prepared to leave Guatemala for Costa Rica in spring 2007 following my meeting at the US Embassy to report the threats I had been receiving, I felt terribly guilty leaving Jorge with no resolution to his daughter's case. Though I did not tell him this, he must have sensed it. He came over one afternoon and said, "Victoria, if I never see you again after you leave, I will always be grateful for all you have done to help me and my beloved Claudina Isabel. I know we will stay in touch." And we did.

From Costa Rica, we continued our conversations and planning via email. Working with Amnesty International UK, I helped organize a public presentation where Jorge could introduce his case to the international community. In May, he wrote to me that the UK trip had been "successful," and he hoped it would "bear fruit in the future." He lamented that "day in and day out, women are being assassinated in Guatemala and the pain of the nation that is bleeding out does not end." Still, he was moved by the response of those who went to his talk. He wrote, "Claudina Isabel has nested permanently in their hearts and become part of their life. She motivates them to struggle for her and for the cause of ending feminicide in Guatemala."[3] I wrote to Jorge that I was working on a book about Claudina Isabel and feminicide that would soon be published in Guatemala.[4]

The Personal Cost of Demanding Justice

In 2007, men and women continued to fall victim to homicide. On August 18, Jorge wrote:

> My Esteemed Victoria,
>   With lament, I inform you that the son of Amílcar Méndez was assassinated yesterday in the afternoon, August 17.
>
>   Jorge.

Jorge's words felt like cold ice running through my veins. I had known Amílcar's son Pepe since he was a little boy when the family was in exile in California. I have photos of him at my home in California when he was maybe 8 years old. The first time I drove by myself up to Nebaj in the Ixil Area, Amílcar had sent then-16-year-old Pepe to accompany me (because I was a woman traveling alone!). But I liked Pepe, and we laughed about his dad's insistence that I needed a male companion to travel safely. The truth is that I had a great trip because Pepe taught me how to 4-wheel-drive through a river when the bridge was out, through deep mud on the shore, and up steep, winding gravel roads with dizzying sheer drops down mountain cliffs. He also drove me home to his mother, who is a nurse, when I inexplicably came down with the mumps during our 1996 trip.

As a child, Pepe survived the grenades thrown at his family's home when his father spoke out for the rights of Indigenous men to not be forcibly conscripted into the Guatemalan army's civil patrols. He helped his father videotape the atrocities and destruction left in the wake of the army's counterinsurgency campaigns. I met him when he accompanied his father to exile in California in the early 1990s. In April 2007, Pepe helped rescue a journalist who had been injured in a rural lynching.

Pepe had worked briefly on a presidential campaign and sometimes accompanied his father to investigate rural human rights violations, but he had tried to build a life outside of his father's work. In 2007, Pepe, son of human rights leader Amílcar Méndez, was working as an air traffic controller at the Guatemala City Airport. He was happily married, with twins. When he was killed, no human rights group would pick up the case because he was not a "human rights defender." I argued with human rights NGO leaders in New York to no avail. I was so angry at the ease with which human rights advocates living in the United States felt it was their right to decide which cases "qualified" under the human rights rubric. I told one that Arthur Helton, founder of the Lawyers Committee on Human Rights, which later became Human Rights First, and who died doing human rights work in Iraq, was rolling over in his grave. Finding no traction with human rights groups or international media, I wrote about Pepe in *Anthropology News*:

> The last time I saw Pepe, he was laughing with his wife, loading their twins into the car, smiling and waving goodbye. But that's not right. On Saturday, I received the terrible news that my friend Pepe Méndez, son of Guatemalan Human Rights Activist Amílcar Méndez, had been brutally assassinated on Friday afternoon on his way home from work. Now I have a photo from last Saturday's news. The car is stopped and the driver's door is open with Pepe's bullet-ridden, bleeding body lying in the middle of a Guatemala City street. Now he is one of the thousands of Guatemalans who have been killed during the decade since the peace accords were signed in 1996.[5]

And thousands more have been killed since Claudina Isabel in 2005 and Pepe Méndez in 2007. Pepe was a victim of impunity and corruption. He had been following aviation guidelines designed to decrease drug trafficking. Pepe was killed for being an honest man and doing his job, a technical job that had nothing to do with human rights but a job that put him directly in conflict with drug trafficking mobsters.

In 2018, Pepe's sister, Ana María Méndez, who had gone to law school with Claudina Isabel, wrote an homage to her brother in *Nomada*:

> I cannot find the words to explain in detail the struggle we have gone through as a family seeking justice for Pepe. It gives me vertigo to remember all the fruitless meetings with the Ministry of the Interior, the endless waiting in the halls of the Prosecutor's Office, the repetitive hearings in tribunals, mob lawyers reading scripts and defending delinquents. My life and my family's life were truncated, marked

with a pause on August 17, 2007, and nothing will ever be the same. The damage is permanent and no sentence will return Pepe. With all my solidarity, I extend this homage to all the victims who, like Pepe, have become one more number in the statistics of impunity for the justice system in Guatemala.[6]

Just as Ana María and Amílcar had joined with Jorge to push for justice for Claudina Isabel, Jorge now joined with them to seek justice for Pepe. This is how organizations of the families of the disappeared were formed in the 1980s. As the numbers of the dead or disappeared climb, so do the numbers of affected families and their collective demand for justice.

Sometimes Jorge would write to me about the pain, always thanking me "for working for the cause of my beloved Claudina Isabel and the women of Guatemala." Sometimes, he found the struggle interminable and difficult. He thought of abandoning the struggle many times, but to do so would be "to renounce her [Claudina Isabel] and become one more Guatemalan without conscience or heart, mediocre, cowardly, hypocritical, apathetic, blind, comatose, vacuous, sick, indifferent and irresponsible." And then as he would begin to surrender to these feelings of powerlessness, he wrote what he often told me: "I hear Claudina Isabel's voice in my heart and she says to me, 'Papi, don't abandon my cause for anything, don't stop struggling for me or for the women in Guatemala. Find strength and be valiant. Don't be afraid and don't lose heart. Search and search again for justice. Pursue it and you will find it.'"

Always, he was gracious and thanked whoever assisted him in his search for justice. In an October 2007 email exchange about different legal strategies, he thanked me for encouraging him and inspiring him to push forward: "You help me see the light at the end of the tunnel, a light that when I reach it will permit me to say to Claudina Isabel, 'my daughter, we have found justice; justice for you, justice for ourselves, justice for Guatemala.'" As always, signed to his atheist friend, "May God bless you, Jorge."[7]

In December, we exchanged family holiday greetings, his more religious than mine. But we both continued working on Claudina Isabel's case. I wrote an article about it for *Harvard ReVista* and promised copies to Jorge when I received them. By mid-January 2008, Jorge was feeling very alone and isolated. He wrote that he missed my company and accompaniment that gave him encouragement and strength, "strength that is constantly abandoning me and pressing me to leave the cause of Claudina Isabel."

Jorge was tired of the loneliness of struggling alone. The family decision with his wife and son was that Jorge would take on this struggle. Claudina's mother would work and support them. Pablo Andrés would continue his studies. These decisions are elaborate calculus formulas seeking to balance the collective mental and emotional health of the family as well as its financial solvency. In Guatemala, the risk of death for raising your voice is also part of the calculus: the fear that whoever killed your loved one will go after another to silence you. In 2007, when I was still in Guatemala, a friend introduced me to her close friend whose 20-year-old son had been killed. The mother was comfortably middle class with some college education. She asked me, "Can you help me?" I asked her if she had gone to the Human Rights Ombudsman or the Prosecutor's Office. I explained the processes for each. Then she said, "But can you help me? Can we find my son's killer without endangering the one who is still alive? Better to remain silent, because I only have one son left now." Everyone knows there is no guarantee. There is risk for oneself and one's loved ones. Jorge was a lone agent with no involvement of his family. That was their only protection. So Claudina Isabel's case was organized like an audit and Jorge's life was organized around this legal and moral pursuit. I felt honored that he would share with me his hope, his fear, his frustration and mirror his experience to me.

"I am tired of struggling without obtaining justice for my beloved and to contemplate the ongoing horror of the women in my country continuing to die before the eyes of an indifferent and irresponsible society that is digging its own grave," he wrote to me. And what you need to understand about Jorge is that these are not platitudes; he feels this horror as he feels the loss of Claudina Isabel. If, as some suggest, pain is an emotion, this frustration and exhaustion is part of his pain. "I am tired of the impunity, injustice, laziness, pain, contempt, and aggression." Having accompanied Jorge and others to many useless meetings with investigators and prosecutors, I certainly shared his exasperation at being "tired of those who put their hopes in power and riches, those who love lies and abandon truth, the cowardly, the vile, the corrupt." Jorge's dedication to finding justice for Claudina Isabel set him apart from these corrupt people and challenged him to hold the course, to not give up. He did not want to become someone who "scorns life and spills innocent blood, who serves himself to the nation that gave us life and does not understand that we are here to serve others, not to be served."

To continue to battle for justice in a system built on impunity designed to wear down the most righteous, Jorge would revert to his lament, to Claudina Isabel's call to his heart. He wrote, "It is only the love of Claudina Isabel that sustains me in this struggle that is so uneven, so unequal, so heartrending and cruel. This is when I hear her beautiful voice that says to me, 'Papi, don't abandon my cause for anything, don't stop struggling for me or for the women in Guatemala. Find strength and be valiant. Don't be afraid and don't lose heart.'" Over the years, I learned that this enduring lament was like a prayer for Jorge to find strength that he would have to seek out over and over again in his often-lone battle against the forces of impunity in Guatemala. Repeating this prayer was revitalizing for Jorge. It overwhelmed him with his daughter's love much in the way that evangelical practices overwhelm celebrants with the sensation of divine presence. Jorge wrote, "The love in me is furious, it roars like a lion, it fills me with force and determination to get around the obstacles that have been placed in front of me—cruel, shady obstacles void of conscience and heart."[8]

When my book *Guatemala: Del genocidio al feminicidio* was published in 2008 in Guatemala, Jorge began to take copies with him wherever he went. In November 2009, he wrote, "Your book about this tragedy has caused a true impact on those who have had the opportunity to read it." He was in Washington, DC, where he had participated in an Inter-American Commission for Human Rights hearing on impunity and human rights violations against women in Guatemala. Four years after the brutal murder of his daughter, he understood her death as part of the "institutionalized killing of women in Guatemala." He told me he missed my accompaniment to the many meetings he endured to push for Claudina Isabel's case, remembering that the meetings with Prosecutors Durán and Matus had been a "true martyrdom," and he likened the meetings he now had with their latest replacement, Blanca Lily Cojulúm, as a "form of torture." He recognized that though there were no real advancements in the case, it remained active because of the national and international pressure we continued to organize to keep Claudina Isabel's case in the public discourse.[9]

Claudina Isabel's Case Goes to the Inter-American Court

In January 2011, almost six years after his daughter's murder, Jorge and Carlos Pop, his lawyer, submitted Claudina Isabel's case to the Inter-American Commission for Human Rights. Pop told me that it was "frustrating" to pursue the case in Guatemala, and at the same time he was "convinced that they had to continue to struggle." He built the case for the Inter-American Commission because the state has responsibility to provide security to its citizens and prevent violence. He felt certain that the case would be accepted because Guatemala would not be able to meet the minimum international requirements of carrying out an effective investigation and determining responsibility for the crime and because of the irregular activities of the government functionaries involved in the investigation. And, like Jorge, he underscored the significance of the case being heard in the international arena because so many women in Guatemala had been killed and nothing had been done to resolve their cases or stop the violence.[10]

As the case went to the Inter-American Court, Jorge insisted on continuing to pressure local authorities and saw small advances in the lines of investigation of Claudina Isabel's murder. These were lines of investigation that, if verified, could lead to identifying suspects. But it would be "a different kettle of fish if the prosecutor could actually formulate charges," and even then it was not clear "if the prosecutors would be able to overcome the many errors made in the investigation."[11]

Though sometimes overwhelmed or discouraged, Jorge pushed to make his daughter's case in every venue to the best of his ability. In 2011, I invited him to be the keynote speaker at a Lehman College conference I organized on gender violence in Central America. Usually a keynote address is about forty minutes, but Jorge needed translation to English, so his time would be cut in half, to twenty minutes. He thanked me for the invitation and lamented that his lack of English provoked a timing problem but insisted he had to have at least thirty minutes to give meaning to his daughter's story and "connect the people at the conference with Claudina Isabel."[12] I gave him thirty minutes (which meant sixty minutes) and scheduled lunch after his talk because I knew he would mesmerize the crowd and get his forty minutes (in Spanish). He took more questions over lunch.

Even though justice was no more in sight in March 2012 than when I first met him five years earlier, I wrote to Jorge, "I hope with all my heart that they investigate and sanction this crime." I also believed that Jorge would find justice in the Inter-American Court, and part of me still believed that he might actually get justice in Guatemala. We continued to knock on all doors and talk to anyone who would listen. And as he struggled with the Inter-American and Guatemalan systems for justice, I acknowledged to him that " a success will be bitter because nothing will bring Claudina Isabel back to life." I told him, "I hear her voice in your voice when you talk about Claudina Isabel. I am sure that now she would say to you, 'Vaya Papi, I knew you could do it.'" The funny thing is that I never met Claudina Isabel. I know her through her father because his love for his daughter is so powerful that he connects you to her.

Not everyone in Guatemala was happy about Jorge's charisma, dedication, and success in taking his daughter's case to the international arena. In May 2012, Jorge received an anonymous email accusing him of being a bad father and responsible for Claudina Isabel's death. The anonymous sender claimed Jorge did not raise her properly, casting aspersions on her character (repeating police and MP investigator statements that she smoked, drank beer, and was not a virgin) and attacking Jorge for not being a forensic expert, accusing him of enjoying his travels to London and the Bronx (where Lehman College is located). The writer suggested he learn English and study criminology instead of imagining what his daughter would say to him. It was a cruel email under the guise of someone seeking his help. Based on the email's content, the sender had access to the police or prosecutor file and knew of his travels. We were never able to determine precisely who was behind this attack. We discussed his options. In the end, Jorge sent me the email to archive. He did not engage with the sender and erased it from his files to eliminate the fury it provoked. It was a cowardly attack. Whoever wrote that email may have had access to the case files, but they certainly did not know Jorge and had clearly never seen him in meetings with the forces of impunity. While Jorge's public presentations could feel like an evangelical revival, he was cool, calm, and fearless in meetings. He embodied Raymond Chandler's hero detective:

> Down these mean streets a man must go who is not himself mean, who is neither tarnished nor afraid. . . . He is the hero, he is everything. He must be a complete man and a common man and yet an unusual man[,] . . . a man of honor, by instinct, by inevitability, without thought of it, and certainly without saying it. He must be the best man in his world and a good enough man for any world.[13]

In early 2013, after eight years of investigating and pushing the Prosecutor's Office to follow up on the case, Jorge wrote that there might be significant movement leading to an arrest, but then I did not hear from him for several months. On August 9, he wrote to me, apologizing for the silence: "We are not doing well. This has been the most difficult year and we are still without solution to so many serious problems." He continued, "I am writing to you because I am feeling very sentimental because this coming week is the anniversary of Claudina Isabel's death. Eight years since she left us, eight years of futile struggle, eight years of arguing her case, eight years of nothing."

Jorge would write to me for support because other friends would tell him to give up, that it was a waste of time, or offer to help eliminate the suspects he had identified. He had to be careful how and to whom he expressed the paradox of seeking justice where there was none. It was a hard balance. He needed to reflect on the profound emotions and frustrations he was experiencing without convincing me to give up. "I continue to insist on justice and push the case forward, but the truth is that I am very tired," he explained. "I feel worn down and I feel like the Prosecutor's Office has achieved its goal of expelling me from the justice system so that I never return." Still, not wanting to lose his faith or mine, he concluded, "The case is still winding through the Commission, I hope they elevate it to the Court."[14]

Seven months later, on March 11, 2014, Jorge wrote to me with great anticipation, "Finally, Good news!!! Claudina Isabel's case has been elevated to the Court!!! It is not public yet, I will let you know when it is." It would be another year before the Inter-American Court would hear the case. On March 4, 2015, Jorge asked me if I could accompany him and his family to Cartagena, Colombia, in April for the Inter-American Court hearing on Claudina Isabel's case. My frustration with the snail-like pace of the process was overrun with elation to see the case finally being heard in the Inter-American Court. Dr. Heather Walsh-Haney, who had provided pro bono forensic review of the case, would also accompany us. It was a haunting moment, ten years after Claudina Isabel's murder. If she had lived, she would have been 29, a practicing lawyer, probably married with children, and Jorge would be a grandfather. Instead, she remains frozen in time, a 19-year-old law student with the world before her when her life was cut short.

That same night, Jorge wrote to me with "joy" that he and his family felt "profoundly supported" because our "accompaniment would provide them with strength and encouragement to continue pushing forward." The renewed participation of the Robert F. Kennedy Center for Justice and Human Rights further buoyed his enthusiasm. Breaking with his conservative and formal writing style, he signed off with, "Big hugs for you and Heather."

Nevertheless, it was hard to pin down the exact date of the hearing during the IAC session, and Jorge was also in the dark about where the IAC session would be held in Cartagena and still waiting for the Robert F. Kennedy Center to tell him where he would be staying. Because Heather and I were covering our travel with our personal funds, we wanted to get advance tickets and a hotel for the best rates. By the time we received the hotel information at the end of the month, we had already made reservations at a hotel recommended by a Colombian friend that turned out to be walking distance from the IAC session location.

Rather than take a direct flight to Cartagena from New York, I flew to Fort Lauderdale to meet up with Heather and fly down together. It was a jubilant flight for us. We had been working on the case for eight years. On that flight, we celebrated that Jorge would have his day in court and Claudina Isabel's case would be heard. And we hoped for justice.

The Extraordinary Session was held at the Cartagena Convention Center (CCC), a modern fortress-like cement square resting on a dock large enough for cruise ships with a palm tree–lined plaza overlooking the Caribbean coast and adjacent to the sixteenth-century colonial walled city. On the roof of the CCC, army sharpshooters in camouflage, wearing large-brimmed green hats with mesh hanging down over their faces, trained their machine guns on potential targets. The colonial port of Cartagena was a major commercial center for the African slave trade and also a seat of the Holy Office of the Inquisition. The IAC hearing was held walking distance from the eighteenth-century Palace of Inquisition and its dungeon. While medieval torture implements were on display for tourists a stone's throw from the CCC, those inside assembled to hear *Velásquez Paiz v. Guatemala*.

Heather and I had to arrive early to line up in the tropical heat to get a seat because no one seemed to know the procedure for us to accompany Jorge, Elsa Claudina, and Pablo Andrés. The line was impressive. Colombian law students from all over the country had traveled to Cartagena to observe the IAC proceedings. Like us, they shared a belief that the IAC could strengthen rule of law in the region. As we passed through security, we entered a dark, cool labyrinth, leaving behind the bright morning sun. We were given a flyer that listed the case with a brief summary on the front and, on the back, the court procedures and names of the judges with a drawing of where each would be sitting. I numbered the bubble drawings of each judge to keep track of their questions in my notes.

"Señoras y Señores, la Corte" (Ladies and Gentlemen, the Court) was announced, and all the spectators obligingly followed protocol, rising from their seats until the judges were seated. As the seven generally gray and balding white male IAC judges from Chile, Peru, Brazil, Colombia, Costa Rica, Uruguay, and Mexico formally filed onto the stage in their flowing black robes, their mostly young, white, female law clerks flurried around them. The lighting created its own anticipation, as lights brightened on the raised stage with the judges and dimmed on the spectator seating of the auditorium. The red, gold, and blue Colombian flag and multicolored OAS flag (containing images of the flags of the thirty-five member nations) flanked the table where the jurists would deliberate. These aging white men who regularly make decisions about human rights violations of marginalized communities of Black, Brown, and Indigenous people in the Americas are representative of the elite white class that produced them. I imagined they often had difficulty relating to the impoverished citizens of the Americas who sought their compassion and adjudication. And, of course, the fact that it was a gendered, all-male tribunal of judges stood out as much as the fact that all of them were white. As I pondered this, I realized they looked just like Jorge and were most likely all fathers as well. And it was impossible not to imagine Claudina Isabel as a law clerk as the young women scurried around them. I leaned over to Heather and said, "Wow, this case is going to be interesting because they can actually relate to the plaintiff and identify with the victim."

The IAC hearing follows a predetermined agenda. First, the Inter-American Commission presents its reasoning and legal argument for bringing the case to the IAC. Next, the Court listens to the victim and their expert and lawyers, followed by closing arguments of the victim's lawyer and the implicated state as well as any final observations from the Inter-American Commission. In turn, the justices ask questions of everyone.

For Santiago Cantón, Inter-American Commission executive secretary and co-counsel, the responsibility for Claudina Isabel's murder rested with the state for failing to protect her life and for failing to take proper and immediate measures to investigate and protect Claudina Isabel after her parents reported her missing. Further, Cantón suggested that the authorities knew full well the context of violence in Guatemala and that she was in imminent danger. They noted that her lifeless body was found the following morning with signs of extreme violence, including sexual violence. Cantón asserted that the state, by its failure to investigate and sanction the murder, had brought IAC scrutiny under international law onto itself. Further, Cantón argued that together the lack of state protection while Claudina Isabel was alive as well as state failure to investigate her murder clearly reflected underlying discrimination against women in Guatemala. Insisting that the protection of all citizens is the obligation and responsibility of the state, Cantón concluded that the state cannot justify its action. Specifically noting gender discrimination, he highlighted the state's continued refusal to recognize or address these problems.

While the lawyers for Jorge, the state, and the Commission all sat at a table facing the justices when it was their turn, Jorge was given a chair set off to the side that faced the justices as well as the spectators sitting in darkness. Jorge wore a light-blue suit and and tie. He was more nervous than I had ever seen him. The lighting made it difficult for him to see all of us sitting in the front row to give him encouragement, and it was all so momentous. But his anxiety melted away as soon as he began to tell the story of his beloved Claudina Isabel—who she was, her life, her family, her aspirations, and then the terrible event that took her life and was relived every time he tried to get the police and prosecutors to do their job. He spoke of the continuous obstacles and the denial of justice, the negligence and inhumanity of the authorities, the way it had drowned him and his family. Then he stopped, looked straight at the justices, and the register of his voice changed as he said, "I have told this story many times, but this is the first time that I present it before a tribunal and I thank you for listening."[15] I was profoundly moved by this statement because my Achi Maya friends from Plan de Sánchez said the same thing when they testified before Judge Santiago Pedraz in the Spanish Tribunal hearing on the Guatemalan Genocide.

Jorge told the story from the night of Claudina Isabel's disappearance, the frantic search to locate her, the refusal by police to even assist them, finding her in the morgue with the help of a friend, having a wake with their family and Claudina Isabel's community of friends when the police burst in, threatening Jorge and demanding access to her body to take fingerprints and nail clippings that should have been taken during the autopsy. I noticed Chief Justice Humberto Antonio Sierra Porto wipe a tear from his eye when Jorge explained, "They defiled the privacy of our family. They handled my daughter's body as if she was a cigar."

Jorge commanded the space. He talked of the constant obstruction of justice, the threats he received. He ticked off the seemingly endless list of deficiencies in the police investigation, the autopsy, and the prosecutor's defiantly dismissive attitude. He described the callous disregard of the authorities for his daughter and the offensive characterizations they consistently used to describe her. "They stigmatized Claudina Isabel as a prostitute, a gang member, a nobody," he declared. He expressed exhaustion with the constant change of prosecutorial guard as her case was moved through Prosecutor's Office 10, 14, 15, and 7, as well as the constant changing of assigned prosecutors in those offices. In the Jefatura de Sección de Delitos contra la Vida (Prosecutor's Office, Homicide Unit) alone, her case had passed through Prosecutors Durán, Matus, and de la Rosa—each fiercely dismissive of the case, yet always faulting Jorge rather than their investigators. "It tears me apart," he lamented. "It is a tempest."

He explained, "They have humiliated me, offended me, aggravated me, insulted my daughter, exhausted me, depleted my energy. They have harmed me. I hear Claudina Isabel say, 'Papi, don't give up your struggle for me.' So we continue. But they have worn us down, they have fractured our family. We are no longer happy. I don't work. But I cannot stop being her father. I am a father demanding and searching for justice."

As if to fully demonstrate Jorge's point about being abused by Guatemalan government prosecutors and proving the deep-seated belief in victim precipitation, Rodrigo Villagrán representing the state began his cross-examination of Jorge: "I want to know about your relationship with your daughter. When did you think your daughter was in danger?" Visibly annoyed, Jorge responded, "I always taught my daughter that we all live in danger, like my son and all children." Villagrán redirected Jorge to his own actions: "What time was late for her to come home?" Jorge redirected the question right back to the night of the murder and briefly repeated the entire sequence of events. Nevertheless, as several justices looked on in visible disbelief, Villagrán insisted that the prosecutors had done their job and that they had also held multiple work meetings with Jorge.

Mexican Justice Eduardo Ferrer Mac-Gregor Poisot asked the first question of Jorge: "What do you hope for from the Court?"

"Sanction Guatemala for the violation of human rights," responded Jorge. "Make them take the necessary steps to stop the killing of women in my country. Parents don't lose their daughters, this state of terror in Guatemala is responsible for the killing."

Scratching his head over the perplexing evidence collection process, Chilean Justice Eduardo Vio Grossi asked about the fingerprints. Jorge explained that they had received Claudina Isabel's body from the morgue after identifying her at 11:00 in the morning. At 9:00 that night, MP Investigative Group 11 arrived at the funeral home. Group 11 was a different investigative group from MP Group 10, which recovered the body from the crime scene and filed the report. But the MP must have falsified the final documents because the autopsy report says the fingerprints and nail clippings were taken by Group 10 at the scene when they were really taken by Group 11 at the funeral home. Justice Vio Grossi then asked, "You authorized them to take the fingerprints?"

Jorge responded, "I authorized them to take the fingerprints under threat. Through my lawyer, the MP said that if I did not permit them to take the fingerprints, they would process me for obstruction of justice. Your Honor, this did not matter to me. What I did not want was for them to defile my daughter's body. When I identified the body of Claudina Isabel in the morgue, the only thing I did was to demonstrate my respect and honor her. I looked at her body covered with a sheet and when I reached her feet, I kissed them. I authorized this process so the MP could not say the case could not move forward because I was an obstacle."

Jorge explained to the IAC justices how he became involved in the case, not just as a parent, but as an investigator and criminologist, effectively carrying out an audit of the system: what the police should have done, what they did and did not do; what the medical examiner should have done, what he did and did not do; what the prosecutors should have done, what they did and did not do. "I never could have done all that I have done on the case if I was not fully dedicated to this," he concluded. The testimony was almost dizzying. Brazilian

Judge Roberto Caldas asked Jorge how the case had affected his life and the life of his family. With great humility, Jorge explained how, "little by little," he went from being an auditor and the primary family breadwinner to working on Claudina Isabel's case full-time—not just eight hours a day, but ten, twelve, or fourteen hours. I had seen this. Jorge breathed the case. It was what got him moving every morning at 5:00 to beat Guatemala City traffic and what kept him up late at night reviewing phone records and responding to the thousands of letters he received from people all over the world through Amnesty International's campaign in support of Claudina Isabel's case. It simultaneously collapsed his life and breathed meaning into his existence.

As Jorge responded to the many reasonable queries from the justices, I thought about how many times he had told this same story to all the police, prosecutors, human rights advocates, ambassadors, consuls, and anyone else who would listen. I remembered a 1997 conversation with Jesús Tec about his experience presenting his childhood survival of the 1982 Río Negro massacre of his community where he witnessed the killing of his mother and siblings and so many others. He told me that he wanted to tell his story so that people know what happened, but it is very hard to stand up and perform because afterward he feels as if it has just happened. How many times do we need to hear the same story to believe its truth?

"This has been so difficult for you and your family," lamented Peruvian Judge Diego García Sayán. "Claudina was a student at the USAC.[16] Was there violence in the USAC?"

"Violence is generalized," explained Jorge. Naming other universities and neighborhoods, he explained, "There is violence in the USAC, Universidad Landívar, Universidad Marroquín, Zone 15, Zone 5, Zone 10. We lived in anguish every day worried about our daughter and the violence as we now worry for our son." Again, he told the story of Claudina Isabel's last night. The party in a nearby neighborhood. Accompanied by her boyfriend. The context of violence then. The continuation of violence now. Women killed, dismembered, raped, beaten in all forms of violation and aggression. "What good is the law if it is not applied?," asked Jorge. "We live in constant fear. We fear for the lives of our women."

"In these ten years, have all these efforts produced any results?," asked Costa Rican Judge Manuel Ventura Robles. "Not exactly," responded Jorge, as he provided another list of incomplete investigations, false starts, and dead ends.

Judge Caldas expressed his perplexity about the use of XX to identify unidentified cadavers. He noted that in other Latin American countries, NN (*ningún nombre*, no name) was commonly used (as is John/Jane Doe in the United States). He asked Jorge if XX was used for all unidentified cadavers in Guatemala or if it had a sexual or gendered connotation. "I am not in capacity to respond to this question because I am not in charge of this. I can tell you that even after we had identified Claudina Isabel, they continued to use XX on her file," Jorge explained.

Colombian Judge Sierra Porto asked Jorge if the violence in Guatemala was generalized violence or if it also involved state actors such as the police. Again with humility, Jorge responded that he couldn't completely answer the question, but he could share his experience and observations.

The violence is generalized, but the Prosecutor's Office does not want to investigate cases, they just want to dispose of them. I was told that there is an order, though I do not know the origin of the order, that all cases from 2010 or earlier are to be archived. What they are interested in is archiving cases and liquidating cases. With this they can make it appear that they are efficient. The impunity in Guatemala is tremendous because the message they send is, "Go kill. Nothing will happen to you." Listen, Your Honor, they assassinated my daughter in the passage of 6 hours. I have spent 10 years trying to get justice for my daughter and I will continue for the rest of my life if I have to do so.

And so it went for another hour and fifteen minutes with questions from the judges and a PowerPoint presentation by the expert witness Claudia González Orellana, beginning with the international human rights of women under the Beijing Platform and the responsibility of the state to carry out adequate criminal investigations. She listed the cause, form, place, and time of death as the minimum requirements to begin an investigation and for the state to fulfill its obligation. She reviewed all the basics of crime scene investigation, autopsy procedures, and basic legal processes. She presented this information within the framework of Claudina Isabel's case. She underscored the importance of the preliminary crime scene investigation in determining the outcome of the legal process. And again, all the phases of the investigation were reviewed against standard investigation procedures, once again revealing the many failures in Claudina Isabel's case. While the Guatemalan government lawyers tried to feign good intentions and reasonable outcomes as they questioned the witnesses, the judges were trying to determine the particularity of Claudina Isabel's case: Was it unique or representative? Chilean Judge Eduardo Vio Grossi focused on González Orellana's testimony that described contamination of the crime scene by the many representatives of diverse government entitities who arrived at the crime scene but failed to effectively collect the evidence as they carried out procedures that were bureaucratic rather than investigative. Judge Vio Grossi wondered if the mishandling of Claudina Isabel's case was an isolated incident.

González Orellana responded that there were numerous studies and reports by various institutions and organizations documenting consistent failures of the state to adequately investigate and sanction femicides. "This is not an isolated case," she explained. Based on her previous work at the Prosecutor's Office, she knew of other cases that were mishandled in the same way. She found similar deficiencies in other cases. She cited the case of Myrna Mack, which she had litigated. "Is this a policy of the state or practice of a state institution?," Judge Vio Grossi asked. "Or is this an isolated case?"

"I believe that the practices of political functionaries seeking to simply complete the forms only because they are required by law converts itself into real deficiencies that the state must address," she answered. "When there are high numbers of cases in impunity without resolution by state institutions, then the state must step in to resolve it."

Judge Ventura Robles of Costa Rica wondered if the police were even competent to carry out the investigation and asked González Orellana if Guatemala was a "failed state"?

"In this case, we can say that the loss of evidence is from the failure of the investigation and the lack of seriousness in pursuing the case, the lack of ongoing coverage of the case, the constant changing of investigators and prosecutors," responded González Orellana. "There is no plan of investigation aimed at gathering evidence to find and prosecute the perpetrator. This is my analysis of the case." She suggested the case lingered as a cold case because key elements were simply not followed to develop lines of investigation. Then the hearing was adjourned until the following day.

On the second and final day of the hearing, Jorge's co-counsel, Kerry Kennedy, president of the Robert F. Kennedy Center for Human Rights, opened with a summary of the importance of Jorge's struggle and Claudina Isabel's case. She thanked Jorge and his family for their decade-long struggle for justice. "Violence against women is the greatest challenge presented to the international community today," she began. "Violence by family, violence by employers, violence by strangers, violence by government officials[,] . . . violence perpetrated against women combatants and civilians during war. And the failure of governments to stop the violence makes structural discrimination all the more pervasive. Across the globe, women who are badgered, beaten, brutalized, mutilated and raped can expect police, judges and prosecutors to humiliate victims, fail to investigate cases and dismiss charges."

Underscoring the significance of Claudina Isabel's case, she reminded the Court, "Worldwide, at least one of every three women—more than two billion women—will be beaten, coerced into sex or otherwise abused in her lifetime. Women constitute half the world's population, perform nearly two-thirds of its work hours, receive one-tenth of the world's income and own less than one-tenth of the world's property."

Kennedy argued that state responses to the killing of women (or lack thereof) is "indicative of the structural discrimination against women." She explained that the result of this discrimination is a "systematic pattern of impunity that perpetuates the cycle of violence by signaling to perpetrators and victims alike that the State tolerates and accepts these heinous crimes." Kennedy's succinct description of outcomes of gender discrimination in Guatemala further reinforces the very tenets of state responsibility for feminicide in Guatemala whether by commission of the crime, toleration of the crime, or omission of state responsibility to investigate and sanction violence against women.

While Carlos Pop had developed the legal arguments specific to Claudina Isabel's case, Kennedy emphasized the magnitude of violence against women beyond Claudina Isabel's case and beyond Guatemala. Kennedy highlighted the importance of this emblematic case and the opportunity presented to the Inter-American Court to establish jurisprudence that would further press governments to address violence against women. Seeking to expand "accountability for the specific failings of the Guatemalan government," she stated, "we are also here to ask this Honorable Court to strengthen the international framework and due diligence obligations of States for the protection of women against femicide and other forms of violence. Doing so will not only help stem the culture of violence in Guatemala, but across the region. And as the jurisprudence of this Honorable Court is often cited in international and domestic tribunals worldwide, this decision could indeed have a ripple effect for women and girls around the globe."

Putting the case at hand in stark relief, Kennedy said, "Claudina Isabel was a promising young law student and future human rights defender whose life was brutally and tragically cut short because she was a woman." Yet in this dark auditorium, Kennedy lifted the mood of the Court: "Claudina Isabel's light is still very much alive and shining; right now, Claudina Isabel's light is filling this room with its brilliance as we come before this Honorable Court to seek justice in her name and on behalf of women worldwide."

Quoting her father, she concluded, "In 1968, the day after Martin Luther King was assassinated in my country, my father, Robert F. Kennedy, spoke about the violence that results from systematic patterns of impunity. He said: 'There is another kind of violence, slower but just as deadly as the shot in the night. This is the violence of institutions; the violence of indifference and inaction and slow decay. . . . Our lives on this planet are too short and the work to be done too great to let this violence flourish any longer in our land.'"

Guatemalan government lawyer, Rodrigo Villagrán, followed Kennedy's moving discourse. He defended Guatemalan state inaction by declaring that there was not enough time for the state to protect Claudina Isabel between her last communication with her parents and her murder. Guatemalan government co-counsel, Steffany Vásquez Barillas, then argued that the Guatemalan state protected the rights of all its citizens based on equality established in the Guatemalan Constitution and therefore did not violate the rights of

Claudina Isabel. Further, she insisted that the state did not discriminate against Claudina Isabel or her family, citing constitutional guarantees of free expression for all Guatemalans as well as the efforts of the Prosecutor's Office in Claudina Isabel's case as evidence.

In disbelief at the willful ignorance of Guatemalan government lawyers, the Inter-American Commission co-counsel, Cantón, said, "It is important to recognize that it has been 15 years since the international community and the Inter-American Court of Human Rights as well as numerous international NGOs have raised awareness of the existence of the epidemic of femicides in Guatemala. The recognition of this epidemic is essential to take action to end this femicide, this continuous massacre of women in Guatemala. It surprises me that the Guatemalan State has not recognized in any moment here the existence of this reality in Guatemala. The Guatemalan State's failure to recognize this, just like the failure through their representatives here in this court, is exactly why there continue to be assassinations of women in Guatemala. Until the State accepts this reality, there will be no modifications or improvements. All the actions that the State mentions are simply formalities."

Significantly, he concluded that the entire apparatus of the state must take action to end violence against women and that simply reciting articles from the Femicide Law was not meaningful protection of the rights of women. Underscoring the need for political will to overcome the bureaucratic proceduralism wherein state action is a formality rather than an application of the law in real time, he stated, "Guatemalan society needs a transformation, and this will not happen simply with the passage of new laws."

In the final few minutes, Carlos Pop methodically contested each of the Guatemalan state's arguments in defense of its inaction, specifically challenging the state for failing to produce any evidence to support its claim that it had protected the rights of Claudina Isabel. He clarified that free expression protected not simply the utterance of words; it protected clothing as a form of free expression as recognized by the United Nations as well as the Inter-American Court, not simply the utterance of words. Specifically, he pointed back to the police officer who stated that the case was not properly developed because Claudina Isabel was wearing sandals and had highlights in her hair and a belly button ring. Pop also challenged the government lawyers who claimed that the crime scene was handled properly. He reminded the Court that the forensic investigators at the crime scene had contaminated evidence because they used Claudina Isabel's sweater to wipe the dirt and blood off her face and then used the same sweater to wipe their own hands. This was the first time I understood why her sweater had been removed at the crime scene. Pop concluded, "Ten years later, and we still do not have the culprits."

Undaunted, Villagrán suggested there was no evidence that the killing of Claudina Isabel was the product of gender violence. As if to prove Santiago Cantón's statement about the Guatemalan state's hallucinatory denial of violence against women and femicide, Villagrán claimed that the government's arguments "are challenging the claims in this specific case, we are not challenging whether or not a generalized condition of violence against women exists."

The Inter-American Commission representative James Louis Cavallaro reiterated the evidentiary and legal reasons that the Inter-American Commission had moved the case forward to the Inter-American Court of Human Rights after thorough review. Cavallaro explained that the case was advanced to the Court because of the state's failure to fulfill its obligation to protect Claudina Isabel Velásquez Paiz's right to life and for violations of judicial guarantees and judicial protections due to the ambience of impunity surrounding the case. He cited the specific context of disappearance and murder known to the state. Cavallaro then reviewed the many errors in the case. The Inter-American Commission followed with summaries of the many institutional failures of the state and the impunity in which the murder took place.

Judge Eduardo Ferrer Mac-Gregor Poisot asked what exactly the state did do to respond to Claudina Isabel's disappearance. "Where does the idea of waiting 24 hours before action on a disappearance come from?"

Making a shadow game of his defense of the state, Villagrán suggested that the statistics on the killing of women were not easily charted because of changes in the law from homicide to femicide. Nevertheless, he went on to claim that the rates of the murders of men in Guatemala were actually higher than the rates of murders of women and that the numbers of men killed had increased more than the numbers of women killed in the same period.[17]

Judge Ventura Robles shook his head in disbelief as he directly asked Villagrán, "Are you telling me that there is no consciousness or concern for this pandemic of femicides in Guatemala?"

Shockingly, Villagrán's response to the Inter-American Court judge was, "No, you are putting words in my mouth. Obviously, there is a concern. . . . We now have prosecutors specifically charged with addressing this problem. But, no, no, we do not consider it to be a pandemic."

Judge Roberto Caldas asked the government lawyers to explain how the state addressed gender in this crime: "Why does the State wait 24 hours to begin investigation? Why does time work against the victims who continue to suffer? Why wouldn't the State act immediately when notified of a crime in progress?" Caldas wanted to know why the Guatemalan state was not proactively developing public policies to stop discrimination against women and also take gender into consideration through state action. Specifically, Caldas asked the government of Guatemala to publicly recognize these issues in their final filing with the Court.

The lawyers were given until May 22, 2015, to respond to questions raised by the Court. To help Jorge's lawyers in their response to the Court, I shared the research and graphs I had made with colleagues that quantify the high levels of violence against women in Guatemala over time. I stayed in touch with colleagues in Costa Rica, always checking in to see if there was any news forthcoming on the case. I emailed Jorge on December 2, 2015, that I had received news that the IAC had rendered its verdict and prior to making it public, would be communicating it first to Jorge and his lawyers as well as the government of Guatemala. I shared my "great hope that the court will take a strong position confronting the barbarity of the state in Claudina Isabel's case and for all the Guatemalan women."

The Sweet Bitter of Justice

The Inter-American Court of Human Rights ruled that Guatemala had an obligation to investigate Claudina Isabel's murder and sanction those responsible. The Court ordered the State of Guatemala to provide medical and psychological assistance to Jorge, Elsa Claudina, and Pablo Andrés. The state was obliged to publish the court's ruling and post it on the webpage of the Ministerio Público for one year. A public apology memorialized in a ceremony with government officials and the participation of the Velásquez Paiz family was to be a symbolic reparation. The Court ordered implementation of permanent and ongoing programs and courses for public functionaries responsible for investigating and sanctioning female homicides, including the courts, the Prosecutor's Office, and the police, on standards of prevention, sanction, and eradication of female homicides as well as trainings in the application of international norms. The Court ordered the Guatemalan state to establish a strategy, system, mechanism, or other national program to achieve the effective and immediate search for disappeared women.[18]

In damages, the family had sought $500,000 for the failure of the state to guarantee the rights of Claudina Isabel. In addition, they had sought $75,000 each for Jorge, Elsa Claudina, and Pablo Andrés for suffering the loss of Claudina Isabel, the anguish and psychological trauma caused by the lack of justice, and the lack of truth about the murder of Claudina Isabel.

The Court ordered the State of Guatemala to pay $60,000 for the intangible damage of losing Claudina Isabel divided equally among Jorge, Elsa Claudina, and Pablo Andrés, with an additional compensation of $18,000 for Jorge, $15,000 for Elsa Claudina, and $12,000 for Pablo Andrés.

The family had also sought $692,424 for the loss of lifetime earnings of Claudina Isabel and $588,031 for Jorge's loss of income resulting from leaving his profession and dedicating himself to investigating her case for ten years. The Court ordered Guatemala to pay $10,000 for Jorge's loss of income and $145,000 for Claudina Isabel's to be divided equally among Jorge, Elsa Claudina, and Pablo Andrés. In addition, the Court ordered the state to pay $9,000 indemnization divided equally among Jorge, Elsa Claudina, and Pablo Andrés.

The family requested $60,000 reimbursement for costs incurred by Jorge in his national and international search for justice. The Court ordered the government of Guatemala to pay Jorge $10,000. For his ten years of labor on the case, the Court ordered the government of Guatemala to pay Carlos Pop $10,000, $5,000 to the Association of Maya Lawyers and Notaries, and $5,000 to the Robert F. Kennedy Center for Justice and Human Rights.[19] In the IAC ruling, the vote is unanimous that the Guatemalan state violated the American Convention on Human Rights Articles 1.1 (Obligation to respect rights and freedoms of the Convention) and 2 (State obligation to adopt rights to give effect to the rights and freedoms of the Convention), as well as Article 4 (Right to Life), Article 5 (Right to Humane Treatment), Article 8 (Right to Fair Treatment), Article 11 (Right to Privacy), Article 25 (Right to Judicial Protection), and Article 7 from the Belém do Pará Convention (State obligation to prevent, punish and eradicate violence against women).

Nonetheless, Judge Caldas of Brazil registered partial dissent and argued that violation of Articles 13.1 (Freedom of Expression) and 22.1 (Freedom of Movement and Residence) should have been included in the ruling. In his six-page dissent, Judge Caldas referenced the police stating that they had judged the value of Claudina Isabel's life and the importance of her case based on her appearance and clothing. This assumption, Caldas argued, is a direct violation of Claudina Isabel's right to freedom of expression because clothing is a fundamental expression of identity. Further, Caldas asserted that the state has the obligation to protect the right of individual expressions of identity regardless of the mode of expression, in this case, clothing and appearance. Further, he asserted the state has a fundamental obligation to ensure a safe environment for women to express themselves. Citing the Inter-American Convention and the International Covenant on Civil and Political Rights, Caldas found the individual choice of clothing integral to freedom of expression whereby one exteriorizes group or cultural belonging; thus individual clothing manifests political significance as well. Caldas's nuanced understanding of clothing as an individual expression and marker of identity reminded me of an Ixil Maya woman friend who told me that she always changed from her traditional huipil and *corte* (traditional Maya skirt) into jeans and a blouse (though it never felt comfortable) to take the bus down the mountains to Guatemala City because she was always treated so poorly by urban Guatemalans when she was wearing her traditional clothing.

Caldas wrote that special protection is required because of the enduring state of macro violence in which women in Guatemala live.

The use of the framework of external appearance—principally clothing—to delegitimize and categorize women inevitably functions to their detriment. Further, Caldas stated that the selectivity of rigor of investigation based on victim clothing reveals the existence of an informal dress code, reinforced by the actions of authorities, that exacerbates the vulnerability of victims. He underscores that women's clothing reflects their belonging to the marginalized female collective simply for choosing to wear outfits that express their identity that are not viewed as appropriate from a patriarchal, machista, or sexist perspective.

Judge Caldas also pointed to the admitted prejudices of investigators based on the location of Claudina Isabel's dead body; the crime scene had been developed with little attention because it was in a "lower-middle-class" neighborhood. Caldas qualified this official attitude as a violation of Claudina Isabel's right to freedom of movement and residence. Caldas compared Claudina Isabel's case to the Toronto, Canada, police response to a 2011 wave of campus sexual assaults on women wherein the police suggested that women should "avoid dressing like prostitutes," thus reinforcing the outdated yet ever-present police framework of victim precipitation. Caldas pointed to Canadian civil society responses defending women's rights to dress as they please and to move freely wherever they wish without risk of being molested, assaulted, or sexually violated. Caldas cited the establishment of the transnational NGO SlutWalk, which challenges the patriarchal gaze on women and asserts their international rights to come and go as they please, as well as their right to freedom of expression through clothing choices. SlutWalk also demanded that men must act within the law, without committing criminal violence against women, and insisted that the state must respect and protect the rights of women.[20]

Caldas argued that dress codes perpetuate sexist gender stereotypes that conceal violence against women and create an environment of impunity for this violence, with an especially "perverse" impact on women, because the state's judgment about the clothing of victims becomes an instrument of state control over women's bodies and justifies the control exercised in supposed "moral values" upheld in communities. In turn, these clothing requirements lend themselves to underlying discriminatory attitudes and allow external control of female sexuality, converting women into objects and denying them autonomy.

By purposefully skipping standard investigative steps and failing to act with due diligence in the criminal investigation, the state ends up penalizing the one who was already victimized—revictimizing the victim. Thus Caldas argued that the state's perspective on the case is itself evidence that women who choose to dress in a certain way lose, though perhaps informally, the right to judicial guarantees for not being considered as "deserving" of these guarantees because of presumed membership in a socially marginalized group of prostitutes or a low socioeconomic class. By expressing their socioeconomic class through clothing, they expose themselves to state inattention and ultimately the violation of some of their rights. Thus, concluded Judge Caldas, "it becomes dangerous to express yourself through clothing and accessories and this danger ends up configured under the right of freedom of expression. It is not possible to fully exercise freedom of expression if some of its manifestations are punished, including in a naturalized way, by the State."[21]

Judge Caldas pointed out that the right to choose to wear or not wear different types of clothing as a form of expression is enshrined in the International Covenant on Civil and Political Rights and that this right of clothing choice should be free of state pressures.[22] Specifically, he cited paragraph 2, in which state signatories (of which Guatemala is one) guarantee that "everyone shall have the right to freedom of expression; this right shall include freedom to seek, receive and impart information and ideas of all kinds, regardless of frontiers, either orally, in writing or in print, in the form of art, or through any other media of his choice." Caldas argued that in this way all forms of expression and their means of diffusion are protected. Beyond the oral and written word, freedom of expression includes nonverbal forms such as images and art objects. Caldas insisted on the significance and breadth of the means of expression, which includes books, newspapers, leaflets, posters, banners, clothing, audiovisual material, electronic news, and the internet. Caldas argued that by failing to guarantee security to all women regardless of what they are wearing, the state ends up having the effect of true prior censorship experienced by women when purchasing or choosing which clothing to wear and how to physically present themselves to the world. Caldas cited a 2014 study in Brazil in which 26 percent of those surveyed agreed that "women who use clothing that shows their body deserve to be attacked."[23] He also cited a UN study on the status of women in Delhi, India, in which 75 percent of men surveyed agreed that "women provoke men by the way they dress."[24]

For Judge Caldas, the link from past to contemporary violence is not lost. Citing *Guatemala: Memoria del silencio,* the Guatemalan truth commission report, Judge Caldas wrote about the extreme human rights violations to which women were subjected during the genocide. Specifically, he linked the "absolute devaluation of women" that permitted army forces to commit violence against women "with total impunity." Notably, he wrote that this process of impunity and devaluation of women did not stop with the end of the war.

To ensure that there would be no misunderstanding of his discussion of women's clothing and rights to free expression, Judge Caldas reiterated that women's clothing is not the cause of violence against women and that women are routinely subjected to violence regardless of their clothing. Rather Caldas's point was that gender preconceptions improperly interfered with the investigation into Claudina Isabel's murder, leaving in stark relief that the potential punishment of aggressors depends on judgments made about the physical appearance of the victim and her clothing: "Effectively, women are not able to express their culture, individuality, ideas or religious affiliations without suffering coercion."

"The implicit message of ineffective investigations in these cases is that a woman expressing dominion over her own body by free choice of clothing can place her in a situation of special vulnerability," Caldas continued. "Judgment of clothing choice impacts respect for women's identity, which is linked to her conception of the world, lifestyle and identification with certain social groups."

Returning to Claudina Isabel's case, Judge Caldas focused on the conduct of the police, who "determined the diligence of the investigation according to guidelines based on the form in which the victim chose to externalize her identity." In the end, police conduct has the effect of pressuring other women to conform to clothing styles deemed "appropriate" under penalty of suffering intensified discrimination. Police references to Claudina Isabel's belly button piercing and sandals exposed her to multiple forms of discrimination, including gender, social condition, age, and economic position. "To link the effective preservation of judicial guarantees to the form in which a woman decides to place herself in the world is a form of preventing the full exercise of freedom of expression and the manifestation of ideas."

Directly challenging the mistaken perspective of the Guatemalan police that a prostitute or gang member does not deserve the same state protection against aggressions and sexual violations, Judge Caldas also underscored that all women deserve and have a right to equal protection.[25]

It is undeniable that clothing is an important, even essential, human expression, whether cultural, national, regional, group, generational, gender, racial, spiritual, or individual. On women's clothing specifically, Judge Caldas wrote that women's choice of clothing is an aesthetic expression that deserves respect.

While alone in his dissenting opinion, Caldas concluded that he wrote this additional ruling of dissent to strengthen the effectiveness of freedom of expression via clothing, as well as freedom of circulation, because these issues had not been previously examined by the IAC. Recognizing the significance of courts of last resort beyond the case under consideration, Judge Caldas explained it was his "hope that national jurisdictions and the actual jurisprudence of this Court will shortly evolve to recognize these rights as fundamental, promoters of real equality among the human genders."[26]

On December 18, 2015, the IAC published its November 19, 2015, ruling on *Velásquez Paiz v. Guatemala*. The Court ordered Guatemala to dedicate resources to prevent violence against women. I congratulated Jorge for his dignified and righteous decades-long struggle for Claudina Isabel. He thanked me for my support and affection. He did not tell me how he felt about the ruling.

The IAC ruling was significant on the jurisprudence front, not only because of the important issues raised in Judge Caldas's dissent about freedom of expression and freedom of movement, but because the Court unanimously agreed that where widespread violence against women is present, the police have a duty to immediately investigate a reported disappearance and that the police had failed to carry out their duties because of discriminatory gender stereotypes. When I asked Carlos Pop what was important about the *Velásquez Paiz* case for confronting feminicide and impunity in Guatemala, he wrote of the great merit of the human rights work of many people in Guatemala, but he emphasized Jorge's unique contribution: "I want to highlight what a father has done in the name of his daughter. I am referring to Jorge Velásquez who has confronted the passivity and aberrant attitude of public functionaries in his search for justice."[27]

At first glance, the IAC ruling appeared fair and just in that it recognized that the Guatemalan state had failed to provide equal protection to Claudina Isabel and sanctioned the government for this failure. There were reparations to be paid to the Velásquez Paiz family, as well as moral and administrative orders from the Court to the Guatemalan government. The decade-long struggle felt like a slow but meaningful victory—a building block in Guatemala's long struggle for equality and rule of law. I was paying more attention to the moral and administrative sanctions than I was to the reparations to the family.

But when I went back over the numbers, I was taken aback by some of the Court's conclusions. For more than ten years, Jorge had dedicated his every waking hour to working on advancing Claudina Isabel's case and calling attention to the killing of women in Guatemala. He had given up his professional work as an accountant to audit the Guatemalan justice system and work on his daughter's homicide case. The family had requested $775,000 for the intangible loss of Claudina Isabel; the Court awarded them $105,000. Jorge had sought $60,000 for the costs of following the case for more than a decade; the Court ordered $10,000 be paid for court costs and $5,000 be paid for travel to the final Inter-American Court hearing in Cartagena. For his loss of earnings for more than a decade, Jorge had requested $588,000; the Court awarded him $10,000—less than $100 a month for the decade of lost work. The family had requested $694,000 for the loss of life earnings of Claudina Isabel based on an expected lifelong career as a lawyer, assuming she would practice as a lawyer for fifty years, from age 25 to 75; the Court awarded $145,000, to be split equally among Claudina Isabel's father, mother, and brother—less than $250 per month over fifty years, much less than the 2019 monthly minimum wage of $357.

While the Court advanced jurisprudence on state responsibility to provide equal protection to all its citizens, it certainly failed to recognize the financial sacrifices made by Jorge to dedicate a decade of his life to seeking justice for Claudina Isabel. Certainly, the Court did not adequately assess the damages suffered by Jorge and his family. Moreover, for a case focused on gender equality, the Court certainly undervalued the social and financial worth of Claudina Isabel's future legal career and what that loss meant for her family.

The feminicide case of Claudina Isabel Velásquez Paiz continues to flounder in the morass of Guatemala's truncated legal system. Indeed, the Inter-American Court condemned the Guatemalan state for its failure to adequately investigate, prosecute, and sanction Claudina Isabel's case and the thousands of other feminicide cases.

In the 2015 ruling in *Velásquez Paiz v. Guatemala,* the IAC ruled that where evidence of widespread violence against women is present, police have a duty to immediately investigate a reported disappearance.[28] The IAC ruling in the *Velásquez Paiz* case is significant because in 2015, ten years after Claudina Isabel's murder, Guatemalan women were no safer, and they are even less safe today. One outcome of the IAC ruling is the Isabel-Claudina Alert system, an Amber Alert for Guatemala, in the name of feminicide victims Isabel Franco and Claudina Isabel Velásquez Paiz. Unfortunately, the police seem satisfied simply to announce an average of four disappearances of women and girls each day;[29] they still do not actually investigate their disappearances. Thus, rather than break the impunity of violence against women in Guatemala, the alert system simply reinforces the normality of daily disappearances of girls and women. Nonetheless, Carlos Pop believes that the decisive enforcement of international court orders such as this IAC ruling compels a reevaluation of the case and the status of the victims seeking justice. In May 2022, nearly seventeen years after Claudina Isabel was murdered, the Prosecutor's Office once again contacted Jorge to review his daughter's murder and perhaps reopen the case. No doubt, to struggle for justice and rule of law in Guatemala, one must suspend cynicism and disbelief to believe in the possibility of transformation.

It is the suspension of cynicism and the shared belief in social transformation and commitment to equality that nurtures David and Goliath struggles for justice. Eduardo Galeano reminded us that *recordar,* "to remember," from the Latin *recorderis,* is to pass back through the heart.[30] In the end, struggles for justice are a practice of righteous memory and a lot like love. Anne Carson wrote *Eros the Bittersweet* about love and the "simultaneity" of its "bitter and sweet."[31] Justice is like love. It is aspirational, incomplete, needed, and potentially healing, requires strength and vulnerability, always reveals an innocence, is a human map of hope. Justice is not easy. Like Jorge's memories of Claudina Isabel, justice is bittersweet.

Notes

Introduction

1. I use "Jane Doe" to protect her identity and that of her family as this is an ongoing legal case in Guatemala.

2. Schlesinger and Kinzer 2005; Kinzer 2013.

3. Burt 2021; Duyos 2021; Falla 1994; Manz 1988.

4. Perera 1971.

5. Argentine Forensic Anthropology Team 1999.

6. Stoll 2019.

7. Lawyer's identity withheld upon request.

8. In 1990 Amílcar Méndez was the recipient of the Robert F. Kennedy Human Rights Award and the Carter-Menil Human Rights Prize. In 1991, he received the Danielle Mitterand Human Rights Award.

9. Ana María Méndez Dardón, email to author, June 5, 2022.

10. This section draws on Victoria Sanford, *Guatemala: Del genocidio al feminicidio* (Guatemala City: F&G Editores, 2008). Courtesy of F&G Editores.

11. This section draws on Victoria Sanford, *Guatemala: Del genocidio al feminicidio* (Guatemala City: F&G Editores, 2008); Victoria Sanford, "From Genocide to Feminicide: Impunity and Human Rights in Twenty-First-Century Guatemala," *Journal of Human Rights* 7, no. 2 (June 14, 2008): 104–22; and Victoria Sanford "Feminicide in Guatemala," *ReVista Harvard Review of Latin America* 7, no. 2 (Winter 2008). Courtesy of F&G Editores and *ReVista Harvard Review of Latin America*.

12. Those 68 murdered girls accounted for 13 percent of female murder victims. PDH 2006.

13. US Department of State 2010.

14. CEH 1999; Sanford 2003b, 2003c.

15. In New York, the murder rate was 4.2 per 100,000. Siff 2022.

16. World Data Atlas 2022.

17. Cooper and Smith 2011.

18. World Bank 2018.

19. PDH 2006, 5.

20. PDH 2006, 9.

21. International Justice Monitor n.d.

22. Quintana Soms 2022.

23. *Rio Times* 2021.

24. Amnesty International 2006.

25. Erturk 2005, 8.

26. Lagarde 2005, 1.

27. Erturk 2005, 10.

28. PDH 2006.

29. Alston 2007, 5–11.

30. Morin 2022.

31. Drinnon 1987.

Chapter 1. The Night Claudina Isabel Did Not Come Home

1. Sections of this chapter have previously appeared in Victoria Sanford, *Guatemala: Del genocidio al feminicidio* (Guatemala City: F&G Editores, 2008); Victoria Sanford, "From Genocide to Feminicide: Impunity and Human Rights in Twenty-First Century Guatemala," *Journal of Human Rights* 7, no. 2 (June 14, 2008): 104–22; and Victoria Sanford, "Feminicide in Guatemala," *ReVista Harvard Review of Latin America* 7, no. 2 (Winter 2008). Courtesy of F&G Editores and *ReVista Harvard Review of Latin America*.

2. Corte IDH 2015a.

3. Ana María Méndez Dardón, email to author, June 5, 2022.

4. Ziomkiewicz, Babiszewska, and Apanasewicz 2021.

5. Clyde Snow, personal communication, July 1, 2006.

6. *Prensa Libre* 2013.

7. De Leon 2015.

8. WikiGuate n.d.

9. Juárez 2018.

10. PNC 2005c.

11. PNC 2005c; MP 2005.

12. Ciani 2005.

13. Reinhard Motte, email to author, August 3, 2016.

14. PNC 2005a.

15. Maldonado Guevara 2005.

16. Author's MP Meeting notes, August 3, 2006.

17. Erturk 2005, 2.

18. Erturk 2005, 9.

Chapter 2. Esperanza's Story

1. Esperanza is a pseudonym; some markers of her identity have been changed to preserve her anonymity.

2. UNDP 2014, 82.

3. Tuckman 2001.

4. Gutiérrez and Kobrak 2001.

5. MINUGUA 2002, 27.

6. Equality Now n.d.

7. National Coalition n.d.

8. Menjívar 2011; Cosgrove and Belisle 2022.

9. Castillo 2016b.

10. Castillo 2016a.

11. This section draws from Victoria Sanford, *Guatemala: Del genocidio al femincidio* (Guatemala City: F&G Editores, 2008). Used with kind permission of F&G Editores.

12. Erturk 2005, 16.

13. CICIG 2018a.

14. Wolfgang 1957.

15. The investigator requested anonymity, including location and date.

16. CICIG 2019.

17. Erturk 2005, 16.

18. Author interview with MP prosecutor requesting anonymity, July 10, 2006.

19. Alston 2007, 5.

20. *La Hora* 2005, 4.

21. Walklate and Fitz-Gibbon et al. 2019.

22. Radford and Russell 1992.

23. Maldonado Guevara, 18.

24. Alston 2007; Erturk 2005.

25. Gartner, Dawson, and Crawford 2001, 160.

26. Gartner, Dawson, and Crawford 2001, 150.

27. Azpuru 2015.

28. Ana María Méndez Dardón, email to author, June 5, 2022.

29. Erturk 2005, 16.

Chapter 3. Cycles of Violence

1. CEH 1999.

2. CEH 1999; Falla 1994; Sanford 2003a.

3. Sanford, Duyos-Álvarez, and Dill 2016, 2020.

4. CEH 1999; Consorcio de Actoras de Cambio 2006, 32.

5. DIA 1991, 3.

6. Ortiz 2004.

7. Magda is a pseudonym; some markers of her identity have been changed to preserve her anonymity.

8. CEH 1999, 310–31; Figueroa Sarti 2012.

9. Posocco forthcoming.

10. SEGEPLAN 2010.

11. US Department of Labor 2020.

12. ILO 2014.

13. ILO 2014.

14. Casaús 2010.

15. SEGEPLAN 2010.

16. UNDP 2014, 52.

17. Velásquez 2017.

18. Thanks to Ana María Méndez Dardón for legal analysis.

19. New America Story Project n.d.

20. Lithwick 2019.

21. CBP Settlement Agreement 2022.

22. Handy 1994; Grandia and Sivaramakrishnan 2012.

23. CEH 1999.

24. CEH 1999.

25. McCreery 1994; Sanford 2009.

26. CEH 1999, 3:891.

27. Miles forthcoming.

28. Deguate 2016.

29. Bloor, Hendry, and Maynard 2006.

30. Karst 1992, 254.

31. Maritza is a pseudonym; some markers of her identity have been changed to preserve her anonymity.

32. Dardón Garzaro 2016.

33. Foucault 1995.

34. Sanford, Duyos-Álvarez, and Dill 2016, 2020.

35. Carolina Escobar Sarti, email to author, June 23, 2016.

36. Women's Link Worldwide 2008.

37. La Coordinación de Acompañamiento 2008; Moran and Paz y Paz Bailey 2005.

38. Women's Link Worldwide 2008.

39. La Coordinación de Acompañamiento 2008.

40. Women's Link Worldwide 2008.

41. Sanford 2000.

42. Sanford 2008a, 2008b.

43. Maldonado Guevara 2005.

44. PDH 2005.

45. FBI 2011; Morgan 2006; UNODC 2019.

46. Piette 2015.

47. Dorian Caal, email to author, April 9, 2015.

Chapter 4. #TengoMiedo (#IAmAfraid)

1. Lidia is a pseudonym; some markers of her identity have been changed to preserve her anonymity

2. Laplace 2015.

3. Musalo and Bookey 2013; INE 2014.

4. Peacock and Beltran 2003.

5. CICIG 2018b.

6. CICIG 2018a.

7. Nichols 2019.

8. CICIG 2018b.

9. Nordstrom 2007.

10. Velásquez 2016.

11. This section draws on Victoria Sanford, "Central America Needs a Regional Commission to Prosecute Corruption, Not a War on Migration," *Barriozona*, May 10, 2021, https://barriozona.com/central-america-migration-guatemala-corruption/. With kind permission from *Barriozona*.

12. Martínez and Labrador 2021.

13. Blitzer 2022; Menchu and Nichols 2018.

14. Blitzer 2022.

15. Sieff 2022.

16. US Border Patrol 2019.

17. Zechmeister and Azpuru 2017.

18. Schneider 2019; US Border Patrol 2019.

19. BBC Mundo 2015.

20. White House Briefing Room 2021.

21. Sanford 2021.

22. The Dialogue 2018.

23. IACHR 2004.

24. Amnesty International 2005b.

25. World Health Organization 2012; Grupo Guatemalteco de Mujeres 2005; Gobierno de Guatemala 2022.

26. Perera 1971, 87.

27. The Guatemalan Forensic Anthropology Foundation (FAFG) has been conducting exhumations of clandestine cemeteries since 1993. It has exhumed hundreds of clandestine cemeteries of massacre victims. The exhumations provide forensic evidence for court cases against military officials and former officials who are the intellectual and material authors of the Guatemalan genocide. See https://fafg.org/.

28. Guatemala Human Rights Commission 2006; Amnesty International 2005a, 2008; Fredy Pecerrelli, email to author, May 25, 2007.

29. Information from human rights activist who requested anonymity to protect the privacy of his niece.

Chapter 5. Paradise for Killers

1. Brookman 2005.

2. Amnesty International 2013.

3. Velásquez Durán 2006.

4. Velásquez Paiz 2007.

5. Velásquez Durán 2006.

6. This section draws on Victoria Sanford, "We've Come for the Garbage," *That Which Remains Journal*, Eric H. Holder Jr. Initiative for Civil and Political Rights, Columbia University, 2 (January 17, 2022), https://www.twrjournal.com /poetry-victoria-sanford.

7. Sanford 2003a.

8. Tom is a pseudonym.

9. US DIA 1990, 33.

10. US DIA 1990, 34.

11. Immigration and Refugee Board 1994.

12. Hemeroteca PL 2018.

13. American Embassy Guatemala 2008.

14. US DIA 1990, 28–29.

15. US DIA 1990, 29.

16. Immigration and Refugee Board 1994.

17. Immigration and Refugee Board 1994.

18. Marlena is a pseudonym.

19. Sanford 2008b.

Chapter 6. Marked Women

1. Manuela is a pseudonym; some markers of her identity have been changed to preserve her anonymity.

2. Sanford 2013.

3. Amnesty International 2005b.

4. UPI 1992.

5. In this section names are withheld and some aspects of identity have been changed to protect the survivors.

6. Rivera was not powerful enough to escape assassination. He was killed on April 7, 2008. Three months later, Juan Carlos Martinez, the prosecutor investigating Rivera's murder, was assassinated. See BBC News, "Gunmen Kill Guatemala Prosecutor," July 15, 2008, http://news.bbc.co.uk/1/hi/world/americas/7506694.stm.

Chapter 7. Bittersweet Justice

1. Sanford 2003b.

2. Burt 2011, 2016, 2019, 2021; Duyos 2021; Dill 2005, 2009.

3. Jorge Velásquez, email to author, May 17, 2007.

4. Sanford 2008b.

5. Sanford 2007.

6. Méndez Dardón 2018.

7. Jorge Velásquez, email to author, October 1, 2007.

8. Jorge Velásquez, email to author, January 17, 2007.

9. Jorge Velásquez, email to author, November 7, 2009.

10. Carlos Pop, email to author, August 1, 2016.

11. Jorge Velásquez, email to author, January 20, 2011.

12. Jorge Velásquez, email to author, January 21, 2011.

13. Chandler 1988, 16.

14. Jorge Velásquez, email to author, August 9, 2013.

15. Audiencia Pública 2015.

16. USAC stands for University of San Carlos in Guatemala City; it is a public institution.

17. While it is true that the number of men killed in Guatemala is higher than the number of women killed, the percentage increase of women killed each year is greater than the percentage increase of men killed. Moreover, worldwide, male homicide victims account for approximately 90 percent of murders, whereas female victims account for less than 10 percent. In Guatemala, female homicide victims account for more than 10 percent of all homicide victims.

18. Corte IDH 2015a.

19. Corte IDH 2015a, 93–98.

20. Corte IDH 2015b.

21. Corte IDH 2015b, 3.

22. See United Nations, International Covenant on Civil and Political Rights, 1966, https://www.ohchr.org/EN/ProfessionalInterest/Pages/CCPR.aspx, article 19.2.

23. For the Brazilian government study of social perceptions, see http://www.ipea.gov.br/portal/images/stories/PDFs/SIPS/140327_sips_violencia_mulheres_novo.pdf. Accessed August 16, 2019.

24. For the UN study of the status of women in Delhi, see http://www.unwomen.org/en/news/stories/2013/2/un-women-supported-survey-in-delhi. Accessed August 16, 2019.

25. Corte IDH 2015b,6.

26. Corte IDH 2015b, 6.

27. Carlos Pop, email to author, August 1, 2016.

28. Corte IDH 2015a.

29. Noticias 7, 2019.

30. Galeano 1991, 11.

31. Carson 1998, 5.

References

Alston, Philip. 2007. "Civil and Political Rights, Including the Questions of Disappearances and Summary Executions." Mission to Guatemala. February 19. United Nations, Human Rights Council. A/HRC/4/20/Add.2.

American Embassy Guatemala. 2008. "Cable 827: Guatemalan Presidential Security Chief Resigns in Wiretapping Scandal." September 14. https://www.scribd.com/document/77077762/Cable-827-Guatemalan-Presidential-Security-Chief-Resigns-in-Wiretapping-Scandal. Accessed June 12, 2022.

Amnesty International. 2005a. "Guatemala: Fear for Safety/Death Threats." September 14. https://www.amnesty.org/en/documents/amr34/038/2005/en/. Accessed June 12, 2022.

———. 2005b. "Guatemala: No Protection, No Justice: Killings of Women in Guatemala." June. https://www.amnesty.org/en/wp-content/uploads/2021/08/amr340172005en.pdf. Accessed June 12, 2022.

———. 2006. "Guatemala: No Protection, No Justice: Killings of Women (an Update)." July 18. https://www.amnesty.org/en/wp-content/uploads/2021/08/amr340192006en.pdf. Accessed September 14, 2022.

———. 2008. "Further Information . . . Fear for Safety/Death Threats." May 21. https://www.amnesty.org/en/wp-content/uploads/2021/06/amr340142008eng.pdf. Accessed June 12, 2021.

———. 2013. "Time to End the Inaction over Killings of Women in Guatemala." January 17. https://www.amnesty.org/en/latest/news/2013/01/time-end-inaction-over-killings-women-guatemala/. Accessed June 12, 2022.

Argentine Forensic Anthropology Team. 1999. "Guatemala: Argentine Forensic Anthropology Team." January 1. http://www.disappearances.org/news /mainfile.php/doc/68/. Accessed June 12, 2022.

Audiencia Pública. 2015. Caso Velásquez Paiz y Otros vs. Guatemala Parte 1. April 28. Parte 1, https://vimeo.com/126508527; Parte 2, https://vimeo .com/126299353. Accessed June 12, 2022.

Azpuru, Dinorah. 2015. "Aprobación de la violencia contra mujeres y niños en Guatemala." *Perspectivas desde el Barómetro de las Américas*, no. 123. https://www.vanderbilt.edu/lapop/insights/IO923es.pdf. Accessed June 11, 2022.

BBC Mundo. 2015. "'La Línea': El que, el cómo y el por qué del escándalo de corrupción que tumbó al presidente de Guatemala." May 8. https://www .bbc.com/mundo/noticias/2015/05/150507_guatemala_corrupcion_ escandalo_vicepresidenta_baldetti_jp. Accessed June 12, 2022.

Blitzer, Jonathan. 2022. "The Exile of Guatemala's Anti-Corruption Efforts." *New Yorker*, April 29. https://www.newyorker.com/news/dispatch/the-exile-of-guatemalas-anti-corruption-efforts. Accessed June 12, 2022.

Bloor, Karen, Vivien Hendry, and Alan Maynard. 2006. "Do We Need More Doctors?" *Journal of the Royal Society of Medicine* 99, no. 6: 281–87. https:// www.ncbi.nlm.nih.gov/pmc/articles/PMC1472715/. Accessed June 11, 2022.

Brookman, Fiona. 2005. *Understanding Homicide*. Washington, DC: Sage.

Burt, Jo-Marie. 2011. "Challenging Impunity in Domestic Courts: Human Rights Prosecutions in Latin America." *Transitional Justice Handbook for Latin America*, edited by F. Reátegui (Brazilian Ministry of Justice and International Center for Transitional Justice), 285–311.

———. 2016. "From Heaven to Hell in Ten Days: The Genocide Trial in Guatemala." *Journal of Genocide Research* 18, no. 2–3: 143–69.

———. 2019. "Gender Justice in Post-Conflict Guatemala: The Sepur Zarco Sexual Violence and Sexual Slavery Trial." Available at SSRN 3444514 (2019).

———. 2021. "The Justice We Deserve: War Crimes Prosecutions in Guatemala." *Latin American Research Review* 56, no. 1: 214–32.

Carson, Anne. 1998. *Eros the Bittersweet*. McLean, IL: Dalkey Archive Press.

Casaús, Marta. 2010. *Guatemala: Linaje y racismo*. Guatemala City: F&G Editores.

Castillo, Mike. 2016a. "Estudiantes se pronuncian en contra de la violencia." *Prensa Libre*, March 3. https://www.prensalibre.com/ciudades/huehuetenango

/estudiantes-se-pronuncian-en-contra-de-la-violencia/. Accessed June 11, 2022.

———. 2016b. "Matan a estudiante por robarle moto en Huehuetenango." *Prensa Libre*, February 22. https://www.prensalibre.com/ciudades/huehuetenango /delincuentes-estropean-sueos-de-superacion-de-estudiante/. Accessed June 11, 2022.

CBP Settlement Agreement. 2022. "Flores v. Garland, Case No. 2:85-cv-4544 (C.D. Cal.), Filed May 21, 2022." https://files.constantcontact.com/baccf499301 /9c4e3ac4-d2a5-44ed-8e49-d586759dfea2.pdf?rdr=true. Accessed June 11, 2022.

Chandler, Raymond. 1988. *The Simple Art of Murder*. New York: Vintage Crime/ Black Lizard.

Ciani, Pedro Adolfo. 2005. "Informe forense del MP." August 30.

Comisión Internacional contra la Impunidad en Guatemala (CICIG). 2018a. "Informe con los resultados obtenidos por el Observatorio Judicial del Sistema de Justicia Penal en Guatemala." https://www.cicig.org /comunicados-2018-c/resultados-obtenidos-por-el-observatorio-judicial -del-sistema-de-justicia-penal/. Accessed June 11, 2022.

———. 2018b. "Mandato y acuerdo CICIG." March 5. https://www.cicig.org /cicig/mandato-y-acuerdo-cicig/. Accessed June 12, 2022.

———. 2019. "Resultados en casos de femicidio y violencia contra la mujer." March 8. https://www.cicig.org/noticias-2019/resultados-en-casos-de- femicidio-y-violencia-contra-la-mujer/. Accessed June 12, 2022.

Comisión para el Esclarecimiento Histórico de Guatemala (CEH). 1999. *Guatemala: Memoria del silencio*. Vols. 1–12. Guatemala City: CEH.

Consorcio Actoras de Cambio. 2006. *Rompiendo el silencio*. Guatemala City: Consorcio Actoras de Cambio y el Instituto de Estudios Comparados en Ciencias Penales.

Cooper, Alexia, and Erica L. Smith. 2011. "Homicide Trends in the United States, 1980–2008." US Department of Justice, Washington, DC. https:// bjs.ojp.gov/content/pub/pdf/htus8008.pdf. Accessed June 9, 2022.

La Coordinación de Acompañamiento Internacional en Guatemala. 2008. "Caso Juana Méndez Rodríguez." http://acoguate.blogspot.com/2008/03 /caso-juana-mendez-rodrguez.html. Accessed June 11, 2022.

Corte IDH. 2004. Caso Masacre Plan de Sánchez vs. Guatemala. Sentencia de 29 de abril. Serie C, No. 105. https://www.corteidh.or.cr/docs/casos /articulos/seriec_116_esp.pdf.

———. 2015a. Caso Velásquez Paiz y Otros vs. Guatemala. Sentencia de 19 de Noviembre de 2015. https://iachr.lls.edu/sites/default/files/iachr/Cases

/Claudina_Isabel_Velasquez_v_Guatemala/004_velasquez_paiz_preliminary_
objections_merits_and_reparations_19nov2015.pdf.

———. 2015b. Voto parcialmente disidente del Juez Roberto F. Caldas. Velásquez
Paiz y Otros vs. Guatemala. Sentencia de 19 de Noviembre de 2015. https://
summa.cejil.org/api/files/15022120093061me93j9kru5iw45m26yhtcsor
.pdf, p.3.

Cosgrove, Serena, and Isabeua J. Belisle Dempsey. 2022. *Imagining
Central America: Short Stories*. Cincinnati, OH: University of Cincinnati
Press.

Dardón Garzaro, Byron. 2016. "Canasta alimentaria aumenta Q382.41." *Prensa
Libre*, May 10. https://www.prensalibre.com/uncategorized/canasta-
alimentaria-aumenta-q38241/. Accessed June 11, 2022.

Deguate. 2016. "Salud en el municipio de San Juan Atitán, Huehuentenango."
https://www.deguate.com/departamentos/huehuetenango/salud-en-el-
municipio-de-san-juan-atitan-huehuetenango/#.V1XCDpErLIU. Accessed
June 11, 2022.

De Leon, Evelyn. 2015. "Guayo Cano ordenó que quemaran a jefe policial de
Salcaja." Soy 502, March 2. https://www.soy502.com/articulo/guayo-cano-
ordeno-quemaran-jefe-policias-salcaja.

The Dialogue. 2018. "Recent Trends in Central American Migration." The
Dialogue—Leadership for the Americas, May 14. https://www.thedialogue
.org/analysis/recent-trends-in-central-american-migration/. Accessed
June 12, 2022.

Dill, K. 2005. "International Human Rights and Local Justice in Guatemala: The
Río Negro (Pak'oxom) and Agua Fria Trials." *Cultural Dynamics* 17, no. 3:
323–50.

———. 2009. "Reparations and the Illusive Meaning of Justice in Guatemala." In
Waging War, Making Peace, edited by Barbara Rose Johnson and Susan
Slymovics, 183–206. New York: Routledge.

Drinnon, Richard. 1987. *Keeper of Concentration Camps: Dillon S. Myer and American Racism*. Berkeley: University of California Press.

Duyos, Sofia. 2021. *Los papeles secretos del genocidio en Guatemala*. Madrid: GPS
Madrid.

EFE. 2008. "Asesinato de fiscal guatemalteco estaría vinculado a caso de
salvadoreños." July 15. http://www.soitu.es/soitu/2008/07/15/info
/1216138929_583141.html. Accessed June 10, 2022.

Equality Now—A Just World for Women and Girls. n.d. https://www
.equalitynow.org/learn_more_child_marriage_us/#:~:text=Child%20

marriage%20is%20currently%20legal,a%20parental%20or%20
judicial%20waiver. Accessed June 11, 2022.

Erturk, Yakin. 2005. "Report of the Special Rapporteur on Violence against
Women, Its Causes and Consequences." United Nations Commission on
Human Rights, Geneva. https://digitallibrary.un.org/record/541832?ln=en.
Accessed June 11, 2022.

Falla, Ricardo. 1994. *Massacres in the Jungle: Ixcán, Guatemala, 1975–1982.*
Boulder, CO: Westview Press.

El Faro. 2007. "Asesor de Vielman tenía estructuras paralelas en El Salvador."
San Salvador.

Federal Bureau of Investigation (FBI). 2011. "Crime Rates in the United States."
https://www.fbi.gov/news/stories/latest-crime-statistics-volumes-continue-
to-fall. Accessed June 11, 2022.

Figueroa Sarti, Raul. 2012. "El 10 de septiembre en nuestra memoria." http://
raulfigueroasarti.blogspot.com/2012/09/el-10-de-septiembre-en-nuestra-
memoria.html. Accessed June 11, 2022.

Foucault, Michel. 1995. *Discipline and Punish: The Birth of the Prison.* Translated
by Alan Sheridan. New York: Vintage Books.

Galeano, Eduardo. 1991. *The Book of Embraces.* New York: Norton.

Gartner, Rosemary, Myrna Dawson, and Maria Crawford. 2001. "Woman
Killing: Intimate Femicide in Ontario, 1974–1994." https://www.research-
gate.net/publication/288867981_Woman_killing_Intimate_femicide_in_
Ontario_1974-1994. Accessed June 11, 2022.

Gobierno de Guatemala. Secretaría Técnica del Consejo de Seguridad Repú-
blica de Guatemala. 2022. "Reportes estadísticas." https://stcns.gob.gt
/reportes/. Accessed June 12, 2022.

Grandia, Liza, and K. Sivaramakrishnan. 2012. *Enclosed: Conservation, Cattle,
and Commerce among the Q'eqchi' Maya Lowlanders.* Culture, Place, and
Nature. Seattle: University of Washington Press.

Grupo Guatemalteco de Mujeres. 2005. "Estudio sobre el femicidio en
Guatemala 2005." https://apps.who.int/iris/bitstream/handle/10665
/77421/WHO_RHR_12.38_eng.pdf. Accessed June 12, 2022.

Guatemala Human Rights Commission. 2006. "Forensic Anthropologists and
Family Members Threatened." January 13. https://www.ghrc-usa.org
/Resources/2006/ForensicAnthropologistsThreatened.htm. Accessed
June 12, 2022.

Gutiérrez, Marta Estela, and Paul Hans Kobrak. 2001. *Los linchamientos pos
conflicto y la violencia colectiva en Huehuetenango, Guatemala.* Guatemala

City: Centro de Estudios y Documentación de la Frontera Occidental de Guatemala (CEDFOG).

Handy, Jim. 1994. *Revolution in the Countryside*. Chapel Hill: University of North Carolina Press.

Hemeroteca PL. 2018. "Estado mayor presidencial: El poder tras el trono." *Prensa Libre,* April 10. https://www.prensalibre.com/hemeroteca/estado -mayor-presidencial-de-guatemala/.

La Hora. 2005. [Blurb.] August 13, 4.

Immigration and Refugee Board of Canada. 1994. "Guatemala: Information on the G-2 Army Intelligence Service." July 1. http://www.refworld.org/docid /3ae6ab9280.html. Accessed June 12, 2022.

Instituto Nacional de Estadística (INE). 2014. *Violencia en contra de la mujer, 2008-2013*. Guatemala City: INE. https://www.ine.gob.gt/sistema/uploads /2014/11/25/ggH7sQs05HbIWZSesco9OUeZqAcHPhYz.pdf. Accessed June 12, 2022.

Inter-American Commission for Human Rights (IACHR). 2004. "Press Communiqué—The IACHR Special Rapporteur Evaluates the Effectiveness of the Right of Women in Guatemala to Live Free from Violence and Discrimination." IACHR, No. 20/04. September 18. http://www.cidh.org /women/Press20.04.htm. Accessed June 12, 2022.

International Justice Monitor. n.d. "Guatemala: Protecting Children from Sexual Violence." https://www.ijm.org/guatemala. Accessed June 9, 2022.

International Labor Organization (ILO). 2014. "Forced Labor: Action to Prevent and Prosecute Human Trafficking in Guatemala." http://www.ilo.org /global/topics/forced-labour/projects/WCMS_320413/lang-en/index .htm. Accessed June 11, 2022.

Juárez, Tulio. 2018. "Suspenden inicio del juicio penal contra 'Guayo Cano' por el asesinato de nueve policías de Salcajá." *El Periódico,* July 5. https:// elperiodico.com.gt/nacionales/2018/05/07/suspenden-inicio-del-juicio- penal-contra-guayo-cano-por-el-asesinato-de-nueve-policias-de-la- pnc-de-salcaja/.

Karst, Kenneth. 1992. *Law and Development in Latin America: A Casebook*. Berkeley: University of California Press.

Kinzer, Stephen. 2013. *The Brothers: John Foster Dulles, Allen Dulles, and Their Secret War*. New York: Times Books.

Lagarde, Marcela. 2005. "Una feminista contra el feminicidio." *Revista Envío* 278.

Laplace, Maria Emilia. 2015. "Internacional: Guatemala tiene la cuarta tasa más alta de femicidios del mundo." *La Izquierdo Diario,* June 24. https://www .laizquierdadiario.com/Guatemala-tiene-la-cuarta-tasa-mas-alta-de-femicidios-del-mundo. Accessed June 12, 2022.

Lawyers' Watch Canada. 2009. "Guatemala Attacks on Jurists." Lawyers' Watch Canada, Vancouver. https://www.lrwc.org/ws/wp-content/uploads/2012 /03/Guatemala.Attacks.on_.Jurists.2005.2009.pdf.

Lithwick, Dahlia. 2019. "Some Did Not Have Socks. Their Hair Was Dirty. An Interview with an Immigration Lawyer Who Visited the Detained Children in Clint, Texas." *Slate,* July 1. https://slate.com/news-and-politics/2019/07 /kids-at-clint-border-crisis-immigration-lawyer-weighs-in.html. Accessed June 11, 2022.

Maldonado Guevara, Alba Estela. 2005. "Femincidio en Guatemala: Crimenes contra la humanidad. Investigación preliminar." November. https://www .corteidh.or.cr/tablas/25828.pdf.

Malkin, Elisabeth. 2010. "2 Top Guatemalan Police Officials Are Arrested on Drug Charges." *New York Times,* March 3, A11.

Manz, Beatriz. 1988. *Refugees of a Hidden War: The Aftermath of Counterinsurgency in Guatemala.* Albany: SUNY Press.

Martínez, Carlos, and Gabriel Labrador. 2021. "Entrevista con un exfiscal rumbo al exilio: 'Todo lo hecho por Porras es oscuro, ahora lo puedo decir.'" *El Faro,* July 25. https://elfaro.net/es/202107/centroamerica/25623/Entrevista-con-un-exfiscal-rumbo-al-exilio-%E2%80%9Ctodo-lo-hecho-por-Porras-es-oscuro-ahora-lo-puedo-decir%E2%80%9D.htm. Accessed June 12, 2022.

McCreery, David. 1994. *Rural Guatemala: 1760–1940.* Stanford, CA: Stanford University Press.

Menchu, Sofia, and Michelle Nichols. 2018. "UN to Send Deputy to Guatemala as Anti-Graft Leader Remains Banned." Reuters, September 19. https:// www.reuters.com/article/us-guatemala-politics/u-n-to-send-deputy-to-guatemala-as-anti-graft-leader-remains-banned-idUSKCN1M003W.

Méndez Dardón, Ana María. 2018. "A mi hermano lo asesinaron por trabajar en el Aeropuerto la Aurora." *Nomada,* August 17. https://nomada.gt/blogs/la-memoria-llama-aunque-la-justicia-no-responda/.

Menjívar, Cecilia. 2011. *Enduring Violence: Ladina Women's Lives in Guatemala.* Berkeley: University of California Press.

Miles, Lesley. Forthcoming. *En Medio, In the Middle.*

Ministerio Público (MP). 2005. *Informe MP001/2005/69430.* August 13 (06:30).

Morán, Ana Lucía, and Claudia Paz y Paz Bailey. 2005. *Cifras de impunidad del crimen policial contra mujeres*. Guatemala City: Instituto de Estudios Comparados en Ciencias Penales de Guatemala.

Morgan, Donna. 2006. "Femicide: The Impact of Victim Offender Relationship on Crime Characteristics." PhD dissertation, City University of New York.

Morin, Brandi. 2022. "Picturesque California Conceals a Crisis of Missing Indigenous Women." *National Geographic*, March 15. https://www .nationalgeographic.com/history/article/california-crisis-missing -indigenous-women. Accessed June 10, 2022.

Musalo, Karen, and Blaine Bookey. 2013. "Crimes without Punishment: An Update on Violence against Women in Guatemala." *Hastings Race and Poverty Law Journal*, no. 10 (Spring): 265–92.

National Coalition to End Child Marriage in the United States. n.d. https:// endchildmarriageus.org/. Accessed June 11, 2022.

New America Story Project. n.d. "Interview: Visiting a Detention Center for Child Immigrants—Professor Bill Ong Hing." https://newamericanstoryproject.org /context/visiting-a-detention-center-for-child-immigrants/. Accessed June 11, 2022.

Nichols, Michelle. 2019. "Guatemala to Shut Down UN Anti-Corruption Body Early." Reuters, January 7. https://www.reuters.com/article/us-guatemala-corruption/guatemala-to-shut-down-u-n-anti-corruption-body-early-id-USKCN1P128Q. Accessed June 12, 2022.

Nonviolent Peaceforce. 2007. "CICIG Opens Dialogue to Establish Its Priorities." http://nonviolentpeaceforce.org/en/guatemalaOct07. Accessed June 3, 2009.

Nordstrom, Carolyn. 2007. *Global Outlaws: Crime, Money, and Power in the Contemporary World*. Oakland: University of California Press.

Noticias 7. 2019. "Diariamente se activan cuatro alertas Isabel Claudina sobre mujeres desaparecidas." March 12. https://www.youtube.com/watch?v= 5VInrLBpClw.

Open Society Institute. 2007. "Community Justice Program." Electronic document. http://www.soros.org/initiatives/baltimore/focus_areas/b_ community. Accessed October 20, 2007.

Ortiz, Dianna. 2004. *The Blindfold's Eye: My Journey from Torture to Truth*. Ossining, NY: Orbis Books.

Peacock, Susan, and Adriana Beltran. 2003. *Hidden Powers: Illegal Armed Groups in Post-Conflict Guatemala and the Forces behind Them*. Washington, DC: Washington Office on Latin America. https://www.wola.org/wp-content

/uploads/2003/09/HiddenPowers-Exec-Summary.pdf. Accessed June 12, 2022.

Perera, Victor. 1971. "Guatemala: Always La Violencia." *New York Times*, June 13, 87.

Piette, Candace. 2015. "Where Women Are Killed by Their Own Family Members." BBC News, December 5. https://www.bbc.com/news/magazine-34978330. Accessed June 11, 2022.

Policía Nacional Civil (PNC). 2005a. *Balística, Informe MP001/2005/69430*. Caso No. 2005-10250557/LB-871005. February 2.

———. 2005b. *Informe 824-05*. Ref/JU.JRMF.ruiz. August 13.

———. 2005c. *Informe No. 2242-2005 EEC G-10*. August 16.

Posocco, Silvia. Forthcoming. *Traces, Remnants, Genocide: Transnational Adoption in Guatemala*.

Prensa Libre. 2009. "Recomienda retirar la imunidad." February 20, A4.

———. 2013. "Matan a ochos policías en Salcajá, Quetzaltenango." June 13. https://www.prensalibre.com/guatemala/justicia/matan-policias-salcaja-quetzaltenango_0_937106568/.

Procuraduría de Derechos Humanos de Guatemala (PDH). 2005. *Informe de muertes violentas de mujeres*. Guatemala City: PDH.

———. 2006. *Informe de las características de las muertes violentas en el país*. February. Guatemala City: PDH.

Quintana Soms, Laura. 2022. "A Lifeline for Survivors of Gender-Based Violence during Lockdown." https://minorityrights.org/trends2021 /guatemala/. Accessed June 9, 2022.

Radford, Jill, and Diana E. Russell. 1992. *Femicide: The Politics of Woman Killing*. Woodbridge, CT: Twayne Publishing.

Reyes, Kenia. 2010. "CICIG da dos hipótesis del plan contra Montenegro." *El Periódico*, March 11. http://www.elperiodico.com.gt/es/20100311/pais /141755/?cat=5.

Rio Times. 2021. "Femicides Increase by 31% in Guatemala during 2021." September 15. https://www.riotimesonline.com/brazil-news/mercosur /central-america/femicides-increase-by-31-in-guatemala-during-2021/.

Roig-Franzia, Manuel. 2007. "Linked Killings Undercut Trust in Guatemala Culture of Corruption, Impunity Exposed." *Washington Post Foreign Service*, March 23, A10.

Russell, Diana, and Roberta Harmes, eds. 2001. *Femicide in Global Perspective*. New York: Teachers College, Columbia University Press.

Sanford, Victoria. 2000. "The Silencing of Maya Women from Mama Maquin to Rigoberta Menchú." *Social Justice* 27, no. 1 (Spring): 128–51.

———. 2002. "Truth Commissions." In *Encyclopedia of Crime and Punishment*, edited by David Levinson, 1637–41. Thousand Oaks, CA: Sage.

———. 2003a. *Buried Secrets: Truth and Human Rights in Guatemala.* New York: Palgrave Macmillan.

———. 2003b. "The 'Gray Zone' of Justice: NGOs and Rule of Law in Post-War Guatemala." *Journal of Human Rights* 2, no. 3 (Fall): 393–405.

———. 2003c. *Violencia y genocidio en Guatemala.* Guatemala City: F&G Editores.

———. 2007. "Memories of a Friend in the Field." *Anthropology News* 48, no. 7 (October): 26.

———. 2008a. "From Genocide to Feminicide: Impunity and Human Rights in 21st Century Guatemala." *Journal of Human Rights* 7, no. 2 (April–June): 104–22.

———. 2008b. *Guatemala: Del genocidio al femincidio.* Guatemala City: F&G Editores.

———. 2008c. "Sí Hubo Genocidio—Yes, There Was a Genocide in Guatemala." In *The Historiography of Genocide,* edited by Dan Stone, 543–76. New York: Palgrave Macmillan.

———. 2009. *La Masacre de Panzós: Etnicidad, tierra y violencia en Guatemala.* Guatemala City: F&G Editores.

———. 2013. "Propaganda, Gangs, and Social Cleansing in Guatemala." In *Virtual War and Magical Death: Technologies and Imaginaries for Killing and Terror,* edited by Neil Whitehead and Sverker Finnstrom, 194–213. Durham, NC: Duke University Press.

———. 2021. "Central America Needs a Regional Commission to Prosecute Corruption, Not a War on Migration." *Barriozona,* May 10. https://barriozona.com/central-america-migration-guatemala-corruption/.

———. 2022. "We've Come for the Garbage." *That Which Remains Journal,* Eric H. Holder Jr. Initiative for Civil and Political Rights, Columbia University, 2 (January 17). https://www.twrjournal.com/poetry-victoria-sanford.

Sanford, Victoria, Sofia Duyos-Álvarez, and Kathleen Dill. 2016. "Women as State Targets: Systematic Gender Violence during the Guatemalan Genocide." In *Gender Violence in Peace and War: States of Complicity,* edited by Victoria Sanford, Katerina Stefatos, et al., 34–46. New Brunswick, NJ: Rutgers University Press.

———. 2020. *Guatemala: Violencia sexual y genocidio.* Guatemala City: F&G Editores.

Sanford, Victoria, and Martha Lincoln. 2010. "Body of Evidence: Feminicide, Local Justice, and Rule of Law in 'Peacetime' Guatemala." In *Transitional Justice: Global Mechanisms and Local Realities in the Aftermath of Genocide and Mass Atrocity,* edited by Alexander Hinton, 67–92. New Brunswick, NJ: Rutgers University Press.

Schlesinger, Stephen, and Stephen Kinzer. 2005. *Bitter Fruit: The Story of the American Coup in Guatemala.* Cambridge, MA: David Rockefeller Center for Latin American Studies.

Schneider, Mark L. 2019. "Democracy in Peril: Facts on CICIG in Guatemala." Center for Strategic and International Studies, April 11. https://www.csis .org/analysis/democracy-peril-facts-cicig-guatemala. Accessed June 12, 2022.

SEGEPLAN. 2010. "Plan de Desarrollo Municipal 2011–2025." http://www .segeplan.gob.gt. Accessed June 11, 2022.

Sieff, Kevin. 2022. "Anti-Corruption Judge Flees Guatemala Despite US Efforts to Protect Her." *Washington Post,* March 21. https://www.washingtonpost .com/world/2022/03/21/guatemala-corruption-judge-erika-aifan/. Accessed June 12, 2022.

Siff, Andrew. 2022. "March Sees Drop in Homicide—but Overall Crime in NYC Spikes over 30%, NYPD Stats Reveal." NBC News New York, April 6. https:// www.nbcnewyork.com/news/local/crime-and-courts/nypd-to-reveal -address-new-york-city-crime-statistics/3633905/.

Stoll, David. 2019. *Rigoberta Menchú and the Story of All Poor Guatemalans.* New York: Routledge.

Tuckman, Jo. 2001. "Mob Justice Kills Eight in Guatemala." *The Guardian,* July 18. https://www.theguardian.com/world/2001/jul/19/jotuckman.

United Nations Development Program (UNDP). 2014. *Memoria Guatemala, 2013–2014.* Guatemala City: UNDP.

United Nations Office on Drugs and Crime (UNODC). 2019. *Global Study on Homicide: Gender-Related Killing of Woman and Girls.* Vienna: UNODC.

United Nations Verification Mission in Guatemala (MINUGUA). 2002. *Los linchamientos: Un flagelo que persiste.* Guatemala City: MINUGUA.

UPI. 1992. "Forensic Specialists Exhume 10 Bodies of Slain Rural Workers." July 29. https://www.upi.com/Archives/1992/07/29/Forensic-specialists- exhume-10-bodies-of-slain-rural-workers/8016712382400/.

US Border Patrol. 2019. "Nationwide Apprehensions by Citizenship and Sector Fiscal Year 2007 to Sept. 30, 2019." Accessed June 12, 2022. https://www .cbp.gov/sites/default/files/assets/documents/2021-Aug/USBORD~3.PDF.

US Defense Intelligence Agency (DIA). 1990. "Intelligence Directorate D-2 of the Guatemalan National Defense General Staff." Secret cable. February 16.

———. 1991. "ESTNA Center Discusses Defense and Security of Guatemala." Conference cable. July 31.

US Department of Labor. 2020. "Child Labor and Forced Labor Reports." https://www.dol.gov/agencies/ilab/resources/reports/child-labor/guatemala. Accessed June 11, 2022.

US Department of State. 2004. *Country Reports on Human Rights Practices 2003: Guatemala.* Washington, DC: Bureau of Democracy, Human Rights, and Labor. February 25.

———. 2010. *Country Report on Human Rights Practices—Guatemala, 2009.* Washington, DC: US Department of State. https://www.refworld.org/publisher,USDOS,ANNUALREPORT,GTM,4b9e52f1c,0.html. Accessed June 9, 2022.

Velásquez, Iván. 2016. "CICIG." Conference Lecture, Woodrow Wilson Center, Washington, DC, April 19.

———. 2017. "Impunity and Institutional Reform in the Guatemalan Post-War: The Impacts of the CICIG." Conference Lecture, University of Guelph, November 3.

Velásquez Durán, Jorge. 2006. Interview by Haroldo Sánchez. *Diálogos con Haroldo Sánchez.* Guatevisión, June 20.

Velásquez Paiz, Pablo Andres. 2007. Interview by Giselle Portnier. In *Killer's Paradise.* Documentary.

Walklate, Sandra, and Kate Fitz-Gibbon, et al. 2019. *Towards a Global Femicide Index: Counting the Costs.* London: Routledge.

White House Briefing Room. 2021. "Vice President Kamala Harris Announces New Commitments as Part of the Call to Action for the Private Sector to Deepen Investment in Central America." December 13. https://www.whitehouse.gov/briefing-room/statements-releases/2021/12/13/vice-president-kamala-harris-announces-new-commitments-as-part-of-the-call-to-action-for-the-private-sector-to-deepen-investment-in-central-america-now-totaling-over-1-2-billion/. Accessed June 12, 2022.

WikiGuate. n.d. "Eduardo Francisco Villatoro Cano." https://wikiguate.com.gt/eduardo-francisco-villatoro-cano/. Accessed June 10, 2022.

Wolfgang, Martin. 1957. "Victim Precipitated Criminal Homicide." *Journal of Criminal Law and Criminology* 48, no. 1 (May–June): 1–12.

Women's Link Worldwide. 2008. "Guatemala, Tribunal de Sentencia Penal, Narcoactividad y Delitos contra el Ambiente, Sentencia C. 26-2007.Of.1a."

April 16. https://www.womenslinkworldwide.org/observatorio/base-de
-datos/sentencia-c-26-2007-of-1a. Accessed June 11, 2022.

World Bank. 2018. "Intentional Homicides (per 100,000 people), 1990–2018."
http://data.worldbank.org/indicator/VC.IHR.PSRC.P5. Accessed June 9, 2022.

World Data Atlas. 2022. "Japan—Homicide Rate." https://knoema.com/atlas
/Japan/Homicide-rate#:~:text=In%202019%2C%20homicide%20rate%20
for,per%20100%2C000%20population%20in%202019. Accessed June 12,
2022.

World Health Organization. 2012. "Understanding and Addressing Violence
against Women." https://apps.who.int/iris/bitstream/handle/10665/77421
/WHO_RHR_12.38_eng.pdf. Accessed June 12, 2022.

Zechmeister, Elizabeth, and Dinorah Azpuru. 2017. "What Does the Public
Report on Corruption, the CICIG, the Public Ministry, and the Constitutional Court of Guatemala?" Latin American Opinion Poll Project, August 31.
https://www.vanderbilt.edu/lapop/insights/ITB029en.pdf. Accessed June
12, 2022.

Ziomkiewicz, A., M. Babiszewska, A. Apanasewicz, et al. 2021. "Psychosocial
Stress and Cortisol Stress Reactivity Predict Breast Milk Composition."
Scientific Reports 11, art. no. 11576 (June 2). https://www.nature.com/articles
/s41598-021-90980-3.

Index

agriculture in Guatemala: child labor, 60–61; Indigenous land usurpation and related violence, 70–72, 96. *See also* plantation agriculture
Aifán, Erika, 92–93
Aldana, Thelma, 92, 94
Aldana Rodríguez, Nery Osberto, 77
Alston, Philip, 14–15, 47
American Convention on Human Rights violations, Claudina Isabel's case and, 158–59, 166
Amnesty International, 13–14, 95, 97, 148
Arbenz, Jacobo, 2
army. *See* Guatemalan army
arranged marriage, 40–41
Arzú, Álvaro, 62–63
autopsies: Claudina Isabel's autopsy, 26–27, 28–29; standard protocols for, 21–22; typical procedure in Guatemala, 24–25. *See also* forensic investigations

Belém do Pará Convention, 159, 166
Biden administration immigration policies and practices, 91, 94
bridewealth, 40

Caal, Dorian, 81
CAFTA (Central America Free Trade Agreement), 88
Caldas, Roberto, 148, 149, 156, 159–64
Cámbara Deras, Luis Ronaldo, 109–10
Canada, femicide in, 49–50
Cano, Guayo, 25
Cantón, Santiago, 144, 154
Carson, Anne, 167
Cavallaro, James Louis, 155–56
CEH (Guatemalan Commission for Historical Clarification), 2, 3, 54, 70–71, 162
Central America Free Trade Agreement (CAFTA), 88
Central American Parliament (PARLACEN) killings, 120, 122, 123
children, 51; child labor, 60–61, 74; child marriage, 43; poor health of Huehuetenango children, 72; rates of violence against, 13, 66; trafficking of, 61, 63; in US border detention facilities, 69–70; as victims of family violence and

children *(continued)*
  sexual abuse, 12, 59–60, 61–62, 82,
    84; as victims/survivors of the
    Guatemalan war and genocide, 3,
    20, 54, 55–56, 57–58
CIACS (Illegal Groups and Clandes-
    tine Security Apparatuses),
    89–90
CICIG (International Commission
    against Impunity in Guatemala),
    46, 88–90, 92, 93–95
Ciudad Juárez, feminicide in, 14
Civil Defense Patrols (PACs), 38,
    39–40, 56, 57, 58
Claudina Isabel's case, 17–35; author's
    involvement with, 6–7, 19–21,
    103–4, 112, 114, 115, 130–31;
    confusion over her identification,
    28–29, 149; confusion over the time
    of death, 26–27, 28–29; the crime
    scene investigation, 10–11, 18,
    25–26, 27, 28, 155, 160; the crime
    scene photos, 8–11; current status
    of, 48, 166–67; dismissive handling
    of the case, 18, 33–36, 53, 79, 99,
    103; events on the night of her
    death, 17–18, 22–23, 145, 147; the
    forensic investigation, 8, 19, 26–32,
    145, 147, 155; her appearance and
    clothing, 9–10, 18, 19, 26, 27, 46,
    159, 160–61; her father's dedication
    to seeking justice, 23, 101–3, 128,
    134–37, 138–41, 146, 148, 164–65;
    her father's interactions with the
    Prosecutor's Office, 32–35, 121–24,
    137, 166–67; her injuries, 9, 10,
    27–28, 29–32; impacts on her family
    and friends, 18–19, 148, 158, 165–66;
    the investigation's deficiencies,
    30–32, 99–101, 145–46, 150–51, 161,
    162–63; leads and potential

suspects, 48, 127–28; media
    attention to, 19–20, 48, 99, 102–3;
    the memorial service, 19, 26, 147;
    public interest and support, 121,
    148; victim precipitation in, 18, 46,
    79, 145, 155, 160; witness inter-
    views, 26, 99–100. *See also*
    Velásquez Durán, Jorge Rolando;
    Velásquez Paiz, Claudina Isabel;
    Velásquez Paiz v. Guatemala
clothing choices: as protected
    freedom of expression, 159–60,
    161–64; victim precipitation based
    on, 18, 46, 159, 160–61
Cojulúm, Blanca Lily, 137
Colom, Alvaro, 109
corporal punishment, 73
Corridor of Violence, 66
corruption, 2, 90–96; anticorruption
    work, 92–95; as context for
    violence in Guatemala, 2, 45, 96,
    110, 130; in the criminal justice
    system, 25, 129, 130, 136; migration
    and, 16, 90–91, 94–95
crime scene investigations: Claudina
    Isabel's case, 10–11, 18, 25–26, 27, 28,
    155, 160; standard protocols for, 21;
    typical procedure in Guatemala,
    23–25
criollos, 62–63
Cruz, Norma, 76
customary law, in Maya communities,
    39

D-2 (Guatemalan Ministry of Defense
    intelligence section), 108–10
DICRI (Department of Criminal
    Investigations), 23–24
disappearances and kidnappings, 2–3,
    51; family support groups and
    justice-seeking organizations, 120,

134. *See also* Guatemalan civil war and genocide

domestic violence: abuse victims' vulnerability to violence, 13; after widowhood, 63; corporal punishment, 73; Esperanza's story, 37, 40–44; Guatemalan men's attitudes about, 82; historical context for, 38–40, 86–87; intimate partner homicide rates, 80–81; Lidia's story, 82–83, 84–86. *See also* intrafamily violence; Magda's story; violence against women in Guatemala

Don Polo (landowner and military commissioner), 71

drug trafficking, 16, 25, 44, 79, 80, 87, 89; the framing of the company president's secretary, 125; Pepe Méndez's killing and, 133

Durán, Renato, 32–33, 33–34, 137, 146

EMP (Presidential General Staff), 108–9

Erturk, Yakin, 35–36, 53

Escobar Sarti, Carolina, 76

Esperanza's story, 37–44; her background and forced marriage, 37, 40–42; her flight from Guatemala and life in the US, 42–43; her return to Guatemala and encounter with her first husband, 43–44; regional violence as context for, 37–40

ethnic groups and hierarchies, 62–63, 64

FAFG (Guatemalan Forensic Anthropology Foundation), 97, 106, 122, 174n27

family violence. *See* domestic violence; intrafamily violence

femicide: as term, vs. feminicide, 48–50

Femicide Law (2008), 65, 69, 154; misapplications/violations of, 65, 67, 68–69, 85

feminicide, as term, 14, 48–50

feminicide in Guatemala: investigation and conviction rates, 46, 47, 66, 83; the Jane Doe case, 3–6, 11, 35; other individual examples, 44–45; social costs of, 14–15; the state's responsibility and impunity analyzed, 151–53, 154; statistics, 11–12, 13, 14, 47, 83, 96; unidentified (XX) victims, 29, 149. *See also* Claudina Isabel's case; state responsibility for violence; victim precipitation; violence against women in Guatemala

forced marriage, 40–41, 43; Esperanza's story, 37, 40–44

forensic investigations: of civil war-era massacres, 97, 106, 107, 122, 174n27; Claudina Isabel's case, 8, 19, 26–32, 145, 147, 155; rape examination protocols and inadequacies, 75–76, 77–78, 80; standard protocols in homicide cases, 21–22, 30, 31–32; typical procedures and inadequacies in Guatemala, 24–25, 80

Foundation Against Terrorism, 93

freedom of expression, 159–60, 161–64

freedom of movement, 42, 43, 53, 117, 159, 160

G-2 (Presidential General Staff intelligence section), 108–9

Galeano, Eduardo, 167

gang activity and violence, 25, 44, 89

gang involvement: attributed to murder victims, 18, 47–48, 79, 95–96, 103; dangers for young women, 116–18; Manuela's story, 118–20

García Sayán, Diego, 148

gender discrimination: clothing and appearance judgments as, 161, 163; as context for violence against women, 13, 14, 45, 57, 152; ethnicity and, 63; state impunity and, 128, 144, 152, 156, 164; victim precipitation and, 95, 161

gender inequality, 12–13, 14; recognition in Guatemala's femicide law, 65

gender violence. *See* violence against women in Guatemala

Giammattei, Alejandro, 91–92, 94

Gómez, Vinicio, 122

González Orellana, Claudia, 150–51

Guatemala City feminicides, 83

Guatemala: Del genocidio al feminicidio (Sanford), 115, 137

Guatemala: Memoria del silencio (CEH report), 162

Guatemalan army: army intelligence and surveillance operations, 107–10; child soldier recruitment, 58; CICIG investigations into illicit activities, 88–90; the civil defense patrols (PACs), 38, 39–40, 56, 57, 58; militarization of Guatemala's borders, 91; role in the Maya genocide, 54–55, 57; as threat to justice operators and peace negotiators, 104–6, 107

Guatemalan civil war and genocide, 2–3, 54–55; the civil defense patrols (PACs), 38, 39–40, 56, 57, 58; as context for increasing family and

gender violence, 39–40, 162; Dianna Ortiz's kidnapping, 56–57; effects on survivors and their children, 2, 55–56, 57–59; forensic investigations of massacres, 97, 106, 107, 122, 174n27; Indigenous land usurpation and related violence, 70–72, 96; the 1996 Peace Accords, 3, 55, 57, 109; Plan de Sánchez massacre, 106, 107, 130, 145; psychosocial impacts of, 2–3, 20, 50–52; sexual violence against Maya women, 55, 75; threats against survivors, 106; US government involvement and intelligence, 2, 15, 56, 108, 109

Guatemalan Commission for Historical Clarification (CEH), 2, 3, 54, 70–71, 162

Guatemalan criminal justice system: access inequities, 39, 44, 45, 78, 83, 86; bureaucratic proceduralism and its impacts, 65–68, 149; dealing with systemic corruption and lawlessness, 88–90, 92–94; dismissive treatment of victims and survivors, 5, 18, 33–36, 53, 84–85, 87–88, 101; investigation and conviction rates for gender violence cases, 46, 47, 66, 83; misapplications/violations of the Femicide Law, 65, 67, 68–69, 85. *See also* Guatemalan police; Prosecutor's Office; state responsibility for violence; victim precipitation; *specific cases*

Guatemalan emigration. *See* migration

Guatemalan ethnic groups and hierarchies, 62–63, 64

Guatemalan Forensic Anthropology Foundation (FAFG), 97, 106, 122, 174n27

Guatemalan genocide. *See* Guatemalan civil war and genocide

Guatemalan government: army surveillance in the National Palace, 109; corruption and anticorruption operators in, 90, 91–93, 94, 95. *See also* state responsibility for violence; *specific branches of government*

Guatemalan law: rape law, 36, 66. *See also* Femicide Law

Guatemalan police: CICIG investigations into illicit police activities, 88–90; distrust/fear of, 25, 42, 43, 79; lynchings of, 4; as perpetrators of violence, 76–78, 79, 120. *See also* Claudina Isabel's case; *other specific cases*

Gutiérrez, Marta Estela, 38

health and health care, 20, 72, 76

Helton, Arthur, 132–33

Hing, Ong, 69–70

Huehuetenango region, 37–38; health care access in, 72; violence in, 38–40, 44–45, 62

human rights advocacy. *See* justice operators and allies; *specific individuals and organizations*

human rights courts and commissions, 129–30. *See also* IAC; IACHR

Human Rights First, 132–33

Human Rights Ombudsman's Office (PDH), 4–5, 106, 112, 123, 128

IAC. *See* Inter-American Court for Human Rights

IACHR (Inter-American Commission for Human Rights), 95, 128, 129–30, 137, 144, 155–56

Illegal Groups and Clandestine Security Apparatuses (CIACS), 89–90

impunity: power, wealth, and the story of the company president's secretary, 124–27. *See also* state impunity

INACIF (National Institute of Forensic Sciences), 24–25, 29, 76

Indigenous people and communities, 37–38; arranged/forced marriage, 40–41; criminal justice access inequities, 39, 44, 45, 78; customary law, 38–39; health inequities and health services access, 72; land usurpation and related violence, 70–72, 96; plantation work and forced labor, 61, 71, 72–73, 74, 78; poverty among, 59, 61, 63, 73–74; regional violence in Huehuetenango, 38–40; as targets of threats and intimidation, 106. *See also* Guatemalan civil war and genocide

infidelity, seen as justification for violence, 51–52

Inter-American Commission for Human Rights (IACHR), 95, 128, 129–30, 137, 144, 155–56

Inter-American Court for Human Rights (IAC), 129–30; Claudina Isabel's case (*Velásquez Paiz v. Guatemala*) referred to, 137; the court's acceptance of the case and hearing, 141–56; the court's rulings, 130, 157–59, 165–66; Judge Caldas's dissenting opinion, 159–64; the significance of the outcomes, 164–67

International Commission against Impunity in Guatemala (CICIG), 46, 88–90, 92, 93–95

International Covenant on Civil and Political Rights, 161–62

Mexico, feminicide in, 14
migration: driving factors, 16, 45, 78, 90, 93, 95; Esperanza's flight, 42–43; Lidia's flight, 85–86; Magda's flight, 69; Manuela's flight, 120; Maritza's flight, 78. *See also* US immigration from Guatemala
MINUGUA (United Nations Mission in Guatemala), 39
misogyny, 12–13, 48–49, 51–52, 53
mob violence: lynchings, 4, 38–39
Morales, Jimmy, 89, 92, 94
Morales Leiva, Brenda, 44–45
Moreno, Zully, 17
Motte, Reinhard, 30, 31–32
MP. *See* Prosecutor's Office
murder rates and statistics, 11–12, 14, 47, 83, 96; deficient handling of statistics, 13–14, 45; male vs. female victims, 156, 176n17
Myer, Dylan S., 15

National Civilian Police (PNC), 45, 88. *See also* Guatemalan police
National Institute of Forensic Sciences (INACIF), 24–25, 29, 76
NGOs: surveillance and intelligence-gathering operations against, 109–10. *See also* justice operators and allies; *specific organizations*

Obama administration immigration policies and practices, 90–91
organized crime, 16, 25, 86, 87; links to state structures and politicians, 44, 89, 94, 96. *See also* gang activity and violence
Ortiz, Dianna, 56–57

Pacific Route CA-02 (Corridor of Violence), 66

PACs (Civil Defense Patrols), 38, 39–40, 56, 57, 58
PARLACEN (Central American Parliament) killings, 120, 122, 123
patriarchy and patriarchal norms: as context for violence against women, 12–13, 39, 57; domestic violence vulnerability and, 59, 61–62, 82–83; gang hierarchies and, 116; in traditional Maya communities, 38–39; victim precipitation and, 50, 52; women seen as needing male protection, 52, 53
Paz y Paz, Claudia, 92, 94
PDH (Office of the Human Rights Ombudsman), 4–5, 106, 112, 123, 128
Pecerrelli, Fredy, 97
Pedraz, Santiago, 130
Pérez Molina, Otto, 94, 95, 96, 108–9
Plan de Sánchez massacre, 106, 107, 130, 145
plantation agriculture: Indigenous land usurpation and related violence, 70–72, 96; Maritza's story, 73–76, 78; owners' and overseers' powers over workers, 71, 72–73, 78
PNC (National Civilian Police), 45, 88. *See also* Guatemalan police
Poisot, Eduardo Ferrer Mac-Gregor, 146, 156
Polanco, Mario, 13
police. *See* Guatemalan police
Pop, Carlos, 123, 128, 137–38, 152, 154–55, 158, 164, 166
Porras, Consuelo, 92–93, 94
Porras, Gloria, 94
Presidential Commission against Corruption, 91, 94
Presidential General Staff (EMP), 108–9

Prosecutor's Office (MP, Ministerio Publico): in Huehuetenango, 44; Jorge Velásquez's interactions with, 32-35, 121-24, 137, 166-67. *See also* Claudina Isabel's case; Guatemalan criminal justice system; state impunity; *other specific cases*

prostitutes, victims profiled as, 18, 46, 47-48, 96, 103, 145, 160

psychosocial impacts of violence, 2-3, 18-19, 20, 50-52; author's experience of intimidation, 104-5, 110-15

Quintanilla, Carlos, 109

racial/ethnic groups and hierarchies, 62-63, 64

Ramos, Sherlyn, 45

rape: in Claudina Isabel's case, 9, 53; examination protocols and inadequacies, 75-76, 77-78, 80; Juana Méndez Rodríguez's story, 76-78; Maritza's story, 73-76, 78; mass rape during the genocide, 55, 75; police as rapists, 76-78, 79; rape law, 36, 66. *See also* sexual violence and abuse

reparations, in IAC cases, 130; *Velásquez Paiz v. Guatemala* rulings, 158, 165-66

restraining orders, 65-66, 67-68, 84-85

Rivera, Victor, 120-21, 122-24, 126, 130, 175n6

rural communities: ethnic hierarchies in, 63; health care and health care access in, 72, 76; typical experiences of rural women and children, 60-61, 62. *See also* Huehuetenango region; Indigenous people and communities

SAAS (Secretariat of Administrative Affairs and Presidential Security), 109

Samayoa Moreno, Pedro, 17

Sánchez, Haroldo, 102

sexual violence and abuse: in Claudina Isabel's case, 9, 53; clothing choices and, 160; during the genocide, 55, 75; Esperanza's story, 41-42; Juana Méndez Rodríguez's story, 76-78; by landowners/overseers, 71-72; Magda's story, 59-60, 61-62; male protection and, 52, 53; Maritza's story, 73-76, 78; marriage as chronic sexual violence, 41-42, 63-64; police as perpetrators of, 76-78, 79; rape examination protocols and inadequacies, 75-76, 77-78, 80; rape law, 36, 66; rates of, 12, 81, 96

Sierra Porto, Humberto Antonio, 145, 149

slavery: marriage as conjugal slavery, 41-42, 63-64

SlutWalk, 160

Smith, Greg, 5, 6

Snow, Clyde, 22, 122

social cleansing, 95-97

state impunity: the CICIG's work against, 46, 88-90, 92, 93-95; dismissive treatment of victims and survivors, 5, 18, 33-36, 53, 84-85, 87-88, 101; gender discrimination and, 128, 144, 152, 156, 164; intimidation of justice operators and, 97-98; role and impacts of, 13-14, 87-88, 149-50, 152-53

state responsibility for violence, 13-14; CIACS (Illegal Groups and Clandestine Security Apparatuses),

victim precipitation (victim blaming or profiling), 36, 160; massacre victims and the disappeared, 3; murder victims, 3, 18, 46–47, 50–52, 79–81, 95, 96, 103, 145, 155, 160; as violation of the Femicide Law, 67–68

Vielman, Carlos, 120, 122, 130

Villagrán, Rodrigo, 146, 153, 155, 156

Vio Grossi, Eduardo, 147, 150, 151

violence against women in Guatemala: driving factors, 12–14; female vs. male homicide rates, 156, 176n17; femicide vs. feminicide, 48–50; historical context for, 38–40, 86–87, 162; investigation and conviction rates, 46, 47, 66, 83; legal access inequities and, 39, 44, 45, 78, 83, 86; patriarchy as context for, 12–13, 39, 57; as retaliation against male relatives, 97–98; the role of state impunity in, 13–14, 87–88, 149–50, 152–53; social costs of, 14–15; statistics and hotspots, 11–12, 13, 62, 66, 96; women who are propositioned by gang members, 116–20. *See also* domestic violence; feminicide; intrafamily violence; sexual violence and abuse; state impunity; state responsibility for violence; victim precipitation; *specific women by name*

violence in Guatemala: as migration driver, 90, 95; the Pavon prison massacre, 91–92; power, wealth, and impunity, 124–27; psychosocial impacts of, 2–3, 18–19, 20, 50–52; social costs of, 14–15, 16; statistics and hotspots, 12, 66, 87; ubiquity of, 4. *See also* Guatemalan civil war and genocide; state impunity; state responsibility for violence; threats and intimidation against justice operators and allies; violence against women in Guatemala

La Violencia. *See* Guatemalan civil war and genocide

Walsh-Haney, Heather, 141, 142

women. *See* feminicide; gender *entries*; misogyny; violence against women in Guatemala

California Series in Public Anthropology

The California Series in Public Anthropology emphasizes the anthropologist's role as an engaged intellectual. It continues anthropology's commitment to being an ethnographic witness, to describing, in human terms, how life is lived beyond the borders of many readers' experiences. But it also adds a commitment, through ethnography, to reframing the terms of public debate—transforming received, accepted understandings of social issues with new insights, new framings.

SERIES EDITOR: IEVA JUSIONYTE (BROWN UNIVERSITY)

FOUNDING EDITOR: ROBERT BOROFSKY (HAWAII PACIFIC UNIVERSITY)

ADVISORY BOARD: CATHERINE BESTEMAN (COLBY COLLEGE), PHILIPPE BOURGOIS (UCLA), JASON DE LEÓN (UCLA), LAURENCE RALPH (PRINCETON UNIVERSITY), AND NANCY SCHEPER-HUGHES (UC BERKELEY)

1. *Twice Dead: Organ Transplants and the Reinvention of Death*, by Margaret Lock
2. *Birthing the Nation: Strategies of Palestinian Women in Israel*, by Rhoda Ann Kanaaneh (with a foreword by Hanan Ashrawi)
3. *Annihilating Difference: The Anthropology of Genocide*, edited by Alexander Laban Hinton (with a foreword by Kenneth Roth)
4. *Pathologies of Power: Health, Human Rights, and the New War on the Poor*, by Paul Farmer (with a foreword by Amartya Sen)
5. *Buddha Is Hiding: Refugees, Citizenship, the New America*, by Aihwa Ong
6. *Chechnya: Life in a War-Torn Society*, by Valery Tishkov (with a foreword by Mikhail S. Gorbachev)
7. *Total Confinement: Madness and Reason in the Maximum Security Prison*, by Lorna A. Rhodes
8. *Paradise in Ashes: A Guatemalan Journey of Courage, Terror, and Hope*, by Beatriz Manz (with a foreword by Aryeh Neier)

Founded in 1893,
UNIVERSITY OF CALIFORNIA PRESS
publishes bold, progressive books and journals
on topics in the arts, humanities, social sciences,
and natural sciences—with a focus on social
justice issues—that inspire thought and action
among readers worldwide.

The UC PRESS FOUNDATION
raises funds to uphold the press's vital role
as an independent, nonprofit publisher, and
receives philanthropic support from a wide
range of individuals and institutions—and from
committed readers like you. To learn more, visit
ucpress.edu/supportus.